BLARNEY CASTLE

Blarney Castle

an Irish tower house

JAMES LYTTLETON

FOUR COURTS PRESS

Typeset in 11 pt on 14 pt ArnoPro by
Carrigboy Typesetting Services for
FOUR COURTS PRESS LTD
7 Malpas Street, Dublin 8, Ireland
www.fourcourtspress.ie
and in North America for
FOUR COURTS PRESS
c/o ISBS, 920 NE 58th Avenue, Suite 300, Portland, OR 97213.

A catalogue record for this title is available
from the British Library.

ISBN 978–1–84682–314–5 pbk

SPECIAL ACKNOWLEDGMENT

This publication received financial support from the Blarney Castle Estate, the Department of
Archaeology at University College Cork, and the National Monuments Service of the
Department of Arts, Heritage and the Gaeltacht.

Printed in Spain
by Castuera, Pamplona

Contents

Preface and acknowledgments

Blarney Castle, the medieval home of the Gaelic Irish lords of Muskerry, is one of Europe's best known castles. Many visitors to Ireland include a visit to the castle in their itinerary, often queuing to kiss the Blarney Stone, in the hope of acquiring the 'gift of the gab'. And yet, despite the castle's ubiquitous image on postcards and tourist promotional literature, there is little acknowledgment of the building's historical and archaeological significance as the chief residence of the lords of Muskerry, a subsidiary branch of the MacCarthy Mór. This book brings the castle's architecture to the fore, placing it in the context of an expansive native lordship in late medieval Munster, and reveals how changes in the layout and appearance of the tower house can be tied in with the social standing and cultural identity of a family whose fortunes waxed and waned through the Tudor reconquest and beyond.

In 2006, the author, working on behalf of the Historic Buildings Survey Unit in the Department of Archaeology, University College Cork, carried out an archaeological and architectural survey of Blarney Castle. This was commissioned by the owner of the castle, Sir Charles Colthurst, in line with recommendations made in a conservation plan for the castle that was prepared by John Cronin and Associates. The survey involved recording all surviving features of archaeological and architectural significance, as well as analyzing relevant published and documentary sources. This allowed for an appraisal of the site's development over time, creating a benchmark on which decisions on the conservation of the castle as it stands today could be made. Part of this work also involved a measured digital survey to provide scaled elevations, floor plans and sections. Focus Surveys Ltd produced the initial elevations, while Hugh Kavanagh, formerly of the Archaeological Services Unit in University College Cork (UCC), created the floor plans and sections.

Thanks, first and foremost, must go to Hugh – his ability and expertise in buildings survey is second to none, and the plans of the castle reproduced in this book are testimony to that. I am also beholden to Dr Colin Rynne, head of the Historic Buildings Survey Unit, who provided much wise advice and counsel during the course of the survey, and whose infectious enthusiasm made the book a reality. I would like to thank the following for their advice and help at various stages: Terry Barry, Karl Brady, Tony Boyle, Fergus Fahey, Aidan Harte, Brian Lacey, Margaret Lantry, Con Manning, Griffin Murray, Tomás Ó Carragáin, Kieran O'Conor, Sara Leggett Painter and Rory Sherlock. I also wish to thank the editor at Four Courts

Press, Michael Potterton, for his much valued guidance in the final stages of preparing the book. Owners of historic sites play a central role in the protection and care of Ireland's archaeological and architectural inheritance, and Sir Charles Colthurst's guardianship of Blarney Castle and Demesne ensures that future generations will continue to enjoy and appreciate the aesthetics and history of this beautiful property. Acknowledgment must be made here of the generous subvention that was made by Sir Charles towards the publication of the work, as well as providing the attractive aerial photographs of the castle and surrounding demesne. I wish to express my thanks to Brian Duffy, Chief Archaeologist of the National Monuments Service, Department of Arts, Heritage and the Gaeltacht, for that body's financial support. Thanks must also go to Tony Roche of the National Monuments Service, Petra Schnabel of the Royal Irish Academy, and Colum O'Riordan of the Irish Architectural Archive for their help in acquiring additional images of Blarney Castle and other sites. Some of the research contained in this book was carried out during my stint as a doctoral student and I wish to express sincere gratitude for the financial support of the Irish Research Council for the Humanities and Social Sciences at the time.

Editorial note

The spellings used for the names of individual MacCarthy lords of Muskerry follow the genealogical listing compiled by Francis J. Byrne in T.W. Moody, F.X. Martin & F.J. Byrne (eds), *A new history of Ireland*, 9 vols (Oxford, 1984), ix, pp 221–2.

Foreword

Blarney Castle is one of the finest and one of the most visited of late medieval castles in Ireland. The great tourist attraction of the Blarney Stone can sometimes lead to visitors not appreciating the fact that they are in an extraordinary heritage building, albeit a ruined one. This book is very welcome especially as it presents the fruits of a recent accurate survey and study of the castle, both of which add greatly to our understanding of the building and those who built it and lived in it. It is written in an authoritative, clear and accessible manner, which will help both the scholar and general reader to place the building in its historical and social context.

The bulk and height of this great tower house with its projecting stone battlements cannot but impress the visitor. I recall seeing it first as a child in the early 1960s and being intrigued and amazed by it. My uncle, Ted Manning, was manager of the estate and on one occasion we stayed with him and his family on our way further west for a holiday. For a child, the mystery of the place with the cave underneath it, the Rock Close and the stories and legends attached to the castle were an added attraction.

This book brings the different phases of the history of Blarney Castle to life – from the original smaller tower house of the MacCarthys of Muskerry in the late fifteenth century, to the greatly enlarged tower house of some decades later, to the early seventeenth-century fortified house, to the Georgian–Gothic mansion of the Jefferyes family in the mid-eighteenth century and finally to the modern estate of the Colthursts. All aspects of the story are of interest, but here the castle itself, possibly the least understood to date, is the main focus.

CONLETH MANNING
Senior Archaeologist
National Monuments Service
18 May 2011

Timeline: twelfth to nineteenth century

(*opposite*) Approaching Blarney Castle from the north through the gardens, a sense of awe is created at the sight of a towering monolith perched on the edge of a rock outcrop. Its walls, built of grey limestone rubble, convey an impression of a foreboding building, dark and dank to live in. Yet, when archaeology and history are combined to recreate the past of such a place, it becomes clear that this was not simply a holdout for embattled MacCarthys, but a lordly residence in which the layout and furnishings displayed the power held by that family.

1495	Eóghan mac Taidhg murders his brother, Cormac 'Láidir', and becomes new lord of Muskerry
1497	John Cabot, on behalf of the English, makes landfall in Newfoundland
1498–1501	Cormac mac Diarmada meic Taidhg, eighth MacCarthy lord of Muskerry
1501–36	Tenure of Cormac Óg Láidir mac Cormaic, ninth lord of Muskerry. During his tenure, the second phase of building takes place, with the extension of the existing tower at Blarney
1509	Henry VII dies and is replaced by his son Henry VIII
1517	Martin Luther exhibits complaints of the Catholic Church in Wittenberg, Germany
1531	Henry VIII is recognized as supreme head of the Church of England
1534–5	The outbreak and suppression of the rebellion of the Anglo-Irish magnates, the Kildare Fitzgeralds, heralds in an era of greater involvement by the English crown in the running of Ireland
1536	Tadhg mac Cormaic Óig becomes tenth lord of Muskerry
1541	Henry VIII of England proclaimed king of Ireland
1542	Tadhg mac Cormaic Óig pledges allegiance to English laws
1547	Henry VIII dies, and is succeeded by his son, Edward VI
1553	Edward VI dies, and is replaced by Catholic monarch, Mary I
1555	Peace of Augsburg in which Lutheranism is recognized in Holy Roman Empire
1556	First English scheme of plantation in Ireland implemented in Cos Laois and Offaly
1558	Queen Mary passes away and is succeeded by Elizabeth I
1565	Sir Diarmaid mac Taidhg becomes eleventh lord of Muskerry
1571	Sir Cormac mac Taidhg becomes twelfth lord of Muskerry
1572	St Bartholomew's Day massacre of French Protestants in Paris
1578	Charter for colonizing Newfoundland granted to Sir Humphrey Gilbert
1579	Earl of Desmond proclaimed a traitor
1583	Ceallachán mac Taidhg becomes thirteenth lord of Muskerry. Earl of Desmond is captured and executed. Sir Humphrey Gilbert takes formal possession of Newfoundland
1584	The estates of the earl of Desmond and his followers are confiscated
1584	Sir Cormac Óg mac Diarmada becomes fourteenth lord of Muskerry
1585	First English colony planted in America at Roanoke Island, North Carolina
1585–6	Plantation of Munster is established
1588	Spanish Armada defeated in the English Channel
1594	Troubles in the north of Ireland evolve into the Nine Years War
1598	The English plantation in Munster is destroyed by Irish rebels

*c.*1600	A new bawn is laid out to the west of Blarney Castle. Square hooded windows replace earlier windows in main chambers. Vault over the 'Banqueting Hall' removed. Chimneystack on top of early tower remodelled
1601	Battle of Kinsale
1603	Elizabeth I dies and is succeeded by James VI of Scotland as James I of England. Treaty of Mellifont ends the Nine Years War, with the earl of Tyrone keeping his estates
1607	Flight of the Earls: earl of Tyrone and earl of Tyrconnell flee to the European continent. First permanent English settlement in America established in Jamestown, Virginia
1609	Plantation scheme for Ulster implemented
1616	Cormac Óg mac Cormaic Óig succeeds as fifteenth lord of Muskerry, created first Viscount Muskerry in 1628
1618	Rebellion in Bohemia leads to Thirty Years War on European continent
1619–20	Plantation schemes implemented for Cos Leitrim, Longford, Westmeath, Offaly and Laois
1625	James I dies and is succeeded by his son Charles I
1631	Baltimore, Co. Cork, sacked by Algerian pirates
1639	Covenanter's rebellion, the first 'Bishops' War' in Scotland against Charles I
Pre-1640	Classical fireplace inserted into first floor room at Blarney Castle. Oriel window inserted into the 'Earl's Bedroom'. Construction of 'new stone house' against the east side of the castle
1640	The second 'Bishops' War' breaks out, results in Treaty of Ripon between Scotland and England
1640	Donnchadh mac Cormaic Óig succeeds as second Viscount Muskerry, created earl of Clancarty in 1658
1641	Outbreak of Irish uprising giving rise to conflict that would last for over a decade
1642	Establishment of the Catholic Confederation of Ireland, and the beginning of the First English Civil War
1643	The last tower house (presently upstanding) in Ireland, built by the O'Maddens at Derryhivenny, Co. Galway
1646	Blarney Castle taken over by parliamentary forces
1648	The outbreak of the Second English Civil War. Peace of Westphalia ends the Thirty Years War on the Continent
1649	End of English Civil War with execution of Charles I. Arrival of Oliver Cromwell and his army into Ireland
1650	Oliver Cromwell departs from Ireland, leaving Henry Ireton in place as deputy
1652	Donnchadh mac Cormaic Óig, Lord Muskerry, is one of the last Catholic leaders to surrender to parliamentary forces, doing so at Killarney, Co. Kerry

1653	End of Irish rebellion and Oliver Cromwell becomes lord protector of Ireland. Blarney Castle is confiscated and granted to Lord Broghill, a Protestant nobleman. Lord Muskerry is exiled to the European continent
1658	In exile, Donnchadh mac Cormaic Óig is created earl of Clancarty. Oliver Cromwell dies and is succeeded by Richard Cromwell as lord protector
1660	Restoration of Charles II to the throne in London
1661	Earl of Clancarty restored to his estates
1665–6	Short tenure of Donnchadh's grandson, Charles James, second earl of Clancarty
1666	Callaghan mac Donnchadha becomes third earl of Clancarty. Great Fire of London breaks out
1676	Donough mac Callaghan becomes fourth earl of Clancarty
1680s	Revd Roland Davis occupies Blarney Castle as tenant
1685	Charles I dies and is succeeded by his brother, James II
1688–9	Outbreak of Glorious Revolution, in which the Catholic James II is deposed and replaced by William of Orange and his wife Mary, daughter of the deposed king. James arrives in Ireland to fight for his cause. Siege of Derry takes place
1690	Jacobite forces defeated at Battle of the Boyne. The earl of Clancarty taken prisoner when city of Cork surrenders to Protestant forces
1691	Jacobite army defeated at Battle of Aughrim, Co. Galway. Treaty of Limerick ends the war in Ireland. Donough mac Callaghan forfeits title and is confined to the Tower of London
1694	Donough mac Callaghan escapes to France
1695	Enactment of penal laws against the Catholic population in Ireland
1697	Donough mac Callaghan returns to England on a visit to his wife. Is arrested and exiled to Germany
1702	Blarney Castle sold by Hollow Sword Blade Company to lord chief justice, Sir Richard Pyne. William III dies and is replaced by Queen Anne. War of Spanish succession commences (ends in 1713)
1703	Sir Richard Pyne sells Blarney Castle to Sir James Jefferyes, governor of Cork city
1707	Union of Scottish and English parliaments
1714	Queen Anne dies and is succeeded by George I
1718	Ulster Scots start to move in significant numbers to America
1720	Collapse of the 'South Sea Bubble'
1722	Captain James Jefferyes inherits Blarney Castle on the death of Sir James
1727	George I dies and is succeeded by George II
1734	Donough mac Callaghan, the last lord of Muskerry, dies in Germany

1739	James St John Jefferyes inherits Blarney Castle on the death of Captain James Jefferyes
1740	Silesia is invaded by Prussia. War of Austrian succession begins (ends in 1748)
1745	Building of Kildare House (later Leinster House, seat of Dáil Éireann) begins
c.1750	construction of Georgian-Gothic mansion on site of older manor house. Large windows inserted into first floor of Blarney Castle, with classical fireplace also partly filled in with brick
1756	Beginning of 'seven years war' between Great Britain and France
1759	Arthur Guinness acquires lease of brewery at St James' Gate, Dublin
1760	George II dies and is succeeded by George III
1765	James St John Jefferyes develops Blarney village as a small manufacturing centre
1776	Declaration of American Independence
1781	Battle of Yorktown in Virginia sees British surrender in the American colonies
1789	Outbreak of the French Revolution
1798	Outbreak of rebellion by the United Irishmen in Ireland
1799	Napoleon Bonaparte takes power in France
1801	Act of Union sees the kingdom of Ireland united with Great Britain
1803	Robert Emmet leads rising in Dublin
1815	Battle of Waterloo in Belgium in which Napoleon Bonaparte is finally defeated
1820	Georgian-Gothic residence at Blarney burnt down. Jefferyes family move to Inishera House in east Cork. George III dies and is succeeded by George IV
1829	Following campaign led by Daniel O'Connell, Catholic emancipation is enacted, allowing Catholics to enter parliament and hold high civil and military offices
1830	George IV dies and is succeeded by William IV
1837	William IV dies and is succeeded by Victoria
1845	Blight destroys potato crop in Ireland, the first of a series of crop failures that results in the Great Famine
1846	With the marriage of Louisa Jane Jefferyes to Sir George Conway Colthurst, the Blarney estate passes to the Colthurst family
1850s	Blarney Woollen Mills established in the village
1862	Start of the American Civil War
1865	Following end of Civil War in the United States, President Abraham Lincoln assassinated
1869	Disestablishment of the Church of Ireland
1874	The Colthursts return to Blarney and build a new Scotch-Baronial residence, designed by John Lanyon, a short distance from the castle

CHAPTER 1

The MacCarthys, lords of Muskerry: their historical pedigree

The MacCarthys in the Middle Ages

Cormac 'Láidir' (the Strong) mac Taidhg MacCarthy, the reputed builder of Blarney Castle (figs 1.1 & 1.3) in the late fifteenth century, came from a noble lineage that went back centuries. The family originated in an area around Cashel, Co. Tipperary, in the eleventh century, minor members of a larger dynastic grouping, the Munster Eóganacht. At this time the MacCarthys were not particularly influential, but in 1118 Turlough O'Connor, contender for the kingship of Ireland, set up the family as rivals to O'Brien dominance in Munster and granted them Desmond, the southern half of Munster.[1] In the early 1130s, a leading member of this dynasty, Cormac MacCarthy, patronized the construction of one of the finest Romanesque chapels in Ireland, on the Rock of Cashel, after having obtained the kingship of Desmond (fig. 1.2).[2] Towards the end of the same century, however, MacCarthy hegemony in southern Munster was greatly shaken by the advent of conquest. The arrival of Anglo-Norman mercenaries in Ireland in 1169 precipitated a series of events, which resulted in the English king, Henry II, declaring himself lord of Ireland. From then on, Ireland's political fate and that of its native aristocracy, was tied to the interests of the English crown. The late twelfth and thirteenth centuries saw the migration of English, Welsh and Flemish settlers into Ireland, where they established, under the auspices of the newly established Anglo-Norman lordships, a network of urban and rural settlement across the country, including lands once held by the MacCarthys.[3]

In the process of resisting these invaders, Diarmait MacCarthy, king of Desmond, was killed at Kilbaun, near Kilcrea, Co. Cork, by the followers of Theobald Walter in 1185. Subsequent Anglo-Norman successes pushed the native lords into the mountainous areas of Kerry in south-west Munster.[4] This allowed for the MacCarthy territory around Cork city to be taken over and parcelled out to various Anglo-Norman lords, including the lands around Blarney, which were granted to the de Guines family. Their moated site and castle can be seen today at Cloghroe, *c.*4km west of Blarney. After a number of decades, though, Anglo-Norman advances in the region were eventually checked at the Battle of Callan, near Kenmare, in 1261, after which the MacCarthys were allowed to consolidate the remnants of their lordship in Kerry.

The zenith of Anglo-Norman expansion was reached by the mid- to late thirteenth century, a time when some of the country's finest castles and churches

1.1 (*opposite*) Blarney Castle, the medieval home of the MacCarthys, lords of Muskerry. The castle is now surrounded by parkland that was laid out by the Jefferyes and Colthurst families in the eighteenth and nineteenth centuries. In the background lies Blarney House, the present residence of the Colthurst family.

1.2 The Rock of Cashel is one of Ireland's best known medieval ecclesiastical sites. In the early 1130s, Cormac MacCarthy patronized the construction of a Romanesque chapel there, after having obtained the kingship of Desmond (© National Monuments Service: Department of Arts, Heritage and the Gaeltacht).

were built.[5] Yet, climatic deterioration, plague, warfare and political infighting among colonial magnates began to undermine the Anglo-Norman colonies in the early decades of the fourteenth century, before they spiralled into decline. For the rest of the fourteenth, and indeed the fifteenth century, the Anglo-Norman colonies succumbed to what has been described as a Gaelic resurgence or revival. This saw the native lords, including the MacCarthys, expanding once more, reclaiming much of their ancestral lands in west and north Cork. This process saw three major branches develop from the principle line of the MacCarthy Mór, who maintained their power base in Kerry. The MacDonagh-MacCarthys of Duhallow laid claim to much of the Blackwater river valley, while the MacCarthys of Muskerry took lands along the Lee and Bride river valleys. The third line, the MacCarthy Reaghs of Carbery, expanded over what remained of west Cork. With increased territory, these branches claimed suzerainty over more minor native families in their expansive lordships including the O'Driscolls, the O'Mahonys, the O'Dalys and the O'Sullivans. The lordship in Muskerry itself was largely defined by the watershed of the River Lee, and extended almost as far as Cork city by the sixteenth century (fig. 1.4).[6]

Where the old Anglo-Norman colonies survived, a hybrid Anglo-Irish culture developed, with both the aristocracy and lower echelons of society borrowing ideals and concepts from their native neighbours, including laws, language and dress. By the end of the fifteenth century, the only area in Ireland where there was effective English governmental control was in the Pale, a territory surrounding the seat of royal administration in Dublin, and in the smaller Wexford Pale, consisting of the baronies of Forth and Bargy. Beyond these heartlands lay a mosaic of autonomous or semi-autonomous lordships under the authority of both Gaelic Irish and Anglo-Irish lords, with the ports on the southern and western coastline, such as Cork, becoming cut off from the centre of crown government and in effect becoming virtually independent city-states. Three of the leading Anglo-Irish families, the Butlers of Ormond, and the Fitzgeralds of Desmond and Kildare, reigned over extensive territories, including palatinates in Tipperary, Kerry and Kildare, which were not answerable to officials in Dublin.[7]

Political discourse in these Anglo-Irish lordships was defined by territorial and military aggrandizement by more robust lords at the expense of weaker ones. The primary allegiance of people within these old colonized areas was to their immediate lords rather than to distant monarchs in England or their nominal representatives. Personal fidelity and mutual protection were the hallmarks of this system, with the most powerful lords maintaining large bands of armed retainers in return for specified payments or exactions.[8] The exercise of authority in these lordships has been characterized as bastard feudalism, which saw magnates expanding their network of dependants beyond traditional territories in a manner that diluted the potential patronage and hence influence of the crown. This could be seen in the Ormond earldom, where client families (from both sides of the ethnic divide) held their lands directly in fee of the earls, in return for fealty, military service, suit of court and a nominal rental charge.[9] Gaelic Irish lordships had also evolved since the fourteenth century to embrace the attributes of feudal lordship. While looking to legitimize their rule by reference to the kingships of the pre-conquest era, the native lords like the MacCarthys in reality exercised their rule differently, in a manner more recognizable to their Anglo-Irish counterparts. Despite the use of traditional inauguration rites, such displays became a mere formality, as election to chiefdom was decided by primogeniture or the exercise of prevailing force. The native lords, with the support of a professional soldiery rather than a hosting of their own free subjects, had little need to consider the wishes of those subjects, except those of their chief vassals. This change in the core relationship between the chief and his people resulted in the terminology of kingship being transformed into discourse revolving around concepts of lordship, ownership in the chief's titles and inauguration rites.[10] Authority was, therefore, not based on a king–subject relationship with every inhabitant in the territory, but on the chief's position as head of the dominant kin group or faction, and on accession to power, he inherited the whole land as demesne, the freeholders who inhabited it being regarded as his tenants.[11]

As mentioned above, the Muskerry MacCarthys expanded eastwards along the Lee river valley and into Blarney on lands at this stage occupied by the de Cogans, an

1.3 Blarney Castle, situated on a rock outcrop in mid-Co. Cork, is Ireland's most famous castle. In late medieval times, this was the domain of one branch of the MacCarthy family, who, as lords of Muskerry, controlled much of the Lee river valley. To the front of the castle are the remains of a Georgian-Gothic mansion, with its distinctive campanile-style round tower, constructed by James St John Jefferyes in the mid-eighteenth century. This replaced an earlier MacCarthy manor house recorded as a 'new stone house' in the 1650s (image courtesy of the Blarney Castle Estate).

1: Tower houses

Crossing the ethnic divide between the Gaelic Irish and the Anglo-Irish, tower houses were a popular type of castle in Ireland. Built between the fifteenth and seventeenth centuries, they were smaller than the earlier Anglo-Norman fortresses, with only a single tower housing most of a lord's household, hence the name – tower house. These buildings were typically four or five storeys in height, and contained one or two chambers on each floor. The massive walls contained additional rooms within their thickness, including toilets, termed garderobes by castle experts. One or two of these floors could be covered by a stone vault, which acted as fireproofing, as well as giving greater structural stability to the building. Access to the various floors was via a single stairwell, in some buildings a straight flight of stairs, in others a spiral stairs. Tower houses were sometimes stand-alone structures, but were more usually surrounded by a walled courtyard known as a bawn (the word deriving from the Irish bádhun – cattle fort – an enclosure where cattle could be corralled). These bawns may only have held cattle in times of emergency, with courtyards typically used to protect ancillary buildings necessary for the running of the lord's demesne and lands. Most of these buildings were built of more perishable material such as timber, post-and-wattle, and clay, and hence have not survived to the present day. These buildings would have included servants' accommodation, as well as kitchens (due to the risk of fire, kitchens were rarely housed within the actual tower houses – Blarney Castle being a notable exception). Another building to be found within the bawn was a great hall, where the lord's household, followers and guests would gather, particularly on ceremonial occasions, when the confines of the tower house were unsuitable for the large numbers of people involved. While tower houses were not designed to withhold against sustained military sieges, a number of defensive features were included, such as arrow loops, yetts (iron grilles placed over doorways), and battlemented walls, which hindered the small-scale raiding that was a feature of life in Ireland in late medieval times.

Anglo-Norman family, who apparently fell into decline in the first half of the fifteenth century. Blarney was now established as one of the main centres of the Muskerry lordship (fig. 1.4).[12] Given the previous history of the native family's dominance in the area before the arrival of the Anglo-Normans, there is a tradition of earlier MacCarthy buildings in Blarney, an eleventh-century hunting lodge and a twelfth-century fortification of stone.[13] This was cited as early as 1837 by Samuel Lewis in his *Topographical dictionary of Ireland*, though such a tradition cannot be substantiated historically and there is certainly no visible archaeological evidence to support this.[14] Many authors have attributed the construction of Blarney Castle in 1446 to one particular MacCarthy lord of Muskerry, Cormac 'Láidir' mac Taidhg, on the basis of a date-stone supposedly inscribed with the following: *Cormac MacCarthaig Fortis me Fieri Facit AD1446*.[15] The same individual was apparently responsible for the construction of the tower house and friary at Kilcrea, just south of the River Lee, *c.*10km west of Ballincollig, as well as another tower house at Carrignamuck in Dripsey (fig. 1.4).[16] However, this date is problematic for both historical and archaeological reasons. Cormac's father, Tadhg mac Cormaic MacCarthy, was still lord of Muskerry in 1446 before eventually being succeeded by Cormac in 1461.[17] Another important consideration is a will made by David Lombard in 1479, a member of an Anglo-Irish merchant family based in Cork city. This document suggests (but does not conclusively establish) that Blarney and Cloghroe were in his hands and a date in the 1480s has been offered as more likely for the construction of Blarney Castle by the MacCarthys.[18] Archaeologically speaking, date-stones, like the Cormac 'Láidir' example, do not normally occur so early as the mid-fifteenth century. Indeed, date-stones only appear in Ireland from the mid-sixteenth century onwards.[19] It has been suggested that the Cormac 'Láidir' date-stone of 1446 may have been added during remodelling carried out by his descendant, Sir Cormac Óg mac Diarmada MacCarthy, as late as the 1590s.[20] Given the evidence above, it is more likely that the castle was initially constructed sometime in the 1480s.[21]

Cormac 'Láidir' mac Taidhg, then, may be regarded as the first occupant of Blarney Castle, though he was slain in 1495 by his brother Eóghan mac Taidhg, who, in turn, was killed and eventually succeeded by Cormac's son, Cormac Óg Láidir mac Cormaic, in 1501 in alliance with the Desmond Fitzgeralds.[22] This MacCarthy lord, however, forestalled the efforts of the Desmonds to assert their rights in Muskerry that had been previously ceded by the de Cogans. In an engagement at Mourne Abbey in mid Co. Cork, the MacCarthys inflicted a serious defeat upon their Anglo-Irish rivals in 1521.[23] By this time, the earls of Kildare (who were also Fitzgeralds), represented the crown's interests in Ireland as lord deputies, and maintained a complex web of political and familial relations with many of the leading Gaelic-Irish and Anglo-Irish nobility across the country. The demise of English rule in Ireland potentially could be exploited by rival powers such as France and Spain, who might seize Ireland, and use it as a means to invade England itself. In addition, the gradual movement of Scots into the north of Ireland also posed a threat to England's

Castles
1 Macroom
2 Carrigadrohid
3 Carrignamuck
4 Blarney
5 Castlemore
6 Kilcrea

20km

1.4 The various MacCarthy lordships, c.1500. In the later medieval period, the MacCarthys reclaimed much of their ancestral lands in Munster that had previously been lost to the Anglo-Normans. This process saw three major branches develop from the principle line of the MacCarthy Mór – the MacDonagh-MacCarthys of Duhallow, the MacCarthy Reaghs of Carbery, and the MacCarthys of Muskerry. Blarney Castle was located in a detached portion of the Muskerry lordship, close to the strategic port city of Cork. Also marked on the map are other important MacCarthy castles in Muskerry (map prepared by Hugh Kavanagh).

2: The MacCarthys

The MacCarthys were one of the leading Irish families in medieval Munster. The family were originally from an area around Cashel, Co. Tipperary, where, in the eleventh century, they were a minor branch of the more influential Munster Eóganacht. In the twelfth century, they grew in political importance, becoming rivals to the O'Briens, and establishing control over Desmond, the southern half of Munster. Later in the same century, their rule in Munster was challenged by the arrival of the Anglo-Normans, who pushed the family into the mountains of Kerry in the south-west. There were limits to this invasion though, and after the defeat of the Anglo-Normans in the Battle of Callan, near Kenmare, in 1261, the MacCarthys were able to consolidate the remnants of their territory in Kerry. With the decline of the Anglo-Norman colonies in the early fourteenth century, the MacCarthys began to reclaim their old lands in west and north Cork, including one branch of the family, the MacCarthys of Muskerry, who reoccupied lands along the Lee and Bride river valleys. Fighting against other native and colonial families, the lords of Muskerry extended their territory quite close to Cork city by the end of the fifteenth century, and it is in this context that Blarney Castle was built on the borders of Muskerry by Cormac 'Láidir' mac Taidhg sometime in the 1480s to defend against territorial encroachment. The MacCarthys of Muskerry were to exhibit equal prowess in the defence of their interests against those of the English crown, as the latter sought to re-establish control over Ireland from the mid-sixteenth century onwards. The family was to survive war and confiscation until their defeat in the Williamite War, known in England as the Glorious Revolution (1689–91). Blarney Castle was confiscated, eventually passing into the hands of the Jefferyes family.

interests.[24] The only solution was to expand governmental control beyond the frontiers of the Pale, and to regain ground in terms of people and territory that had been lost over the previous two centuries. The English government under Henry VIII began to reassert itself, pushing the Kildare Fitzgeralds into rebellion and eventual defeat in 1534–5. From then on, only men born in England were now called to the office of lord deputy, to act as the crown's highest representative in Ireland, and this was to have implications for the native lords, including the MacCarthys of Muskerry.[25]

The decline of MacCarthy power

The first step in countering the native Irish and Anglo-Irish lordships was the proclamation of Henry VIII as king of Ireland in 1541, an elevation from his previous title as lord of Ireland. This created a legal basis for the political unification of the country, which had up until then been effectively partitioned between areas where English common law was practised and those areas that hitherto followed native concepts of law and order.[26] Anglo-Irish commentators argued that the reform of Gaelic society could be brought about by the persuasion of the nobility of that society to undergo an educational process to follow civil standards as practised in more anglicized parts of the country. Such a belief was given practical application with the 'surrender and regrant' scheme in the 1540s.[27] Under the policy of surrender and regrant, the native lords surrendered their lordships to the crown, upon which their traditional lands would be granted back to be held of the crown under English title. This in effect bequeathed the status of landed nobility and gentry to the native landowners, establishing greater security to their lordships with the support of the crown. In most instances, the reinstated lords were obliged to abandon their military ways, forego the traditional payments and exactions that their dynasties had hitherto enjoyed, and facilitate the gradual anglicization of their lordships by having their nominated heirs raised in the households of English gentlemen either in the Pale or in England. The flip side of this arrangement, however, was that in the event of rebellion by the same landowners, their lands and entitlements could be rendered forfeit to the crown, a situation that was to be exploited by English officialdom in years to come.[28] In 1542, Tadhg mac Cormaic Óig MacCarthy along with other Irish native lords pledged allegiance to English laws; and in 1558, his son Diarmaid mac Taidhg was knighted in Limerick on his submission to the crown.[29]

The sixteenth century was hence an anxious time for the native elite, whose power-base was under threat from the expansionist tendencies of a Tudor state that sought to re-establish control over the semi-autonomous lordships. It is clear that the lords of Muskerry sought to negotiate their political and social coherence in these unsettled times. One MacCarthy lord (who also happened to be knighted in the English manner), Sir Cormac mac Taidhg, was complimented in 1575 by the lord deputy, Sir Henry Sidney, for being 'the rarest man that ever was born of the Irishry'.

Indeed his own son, Cormac Óg, acted as page to Sir Walter Raleigh for a time.[30] The construction of tower houses like Blarney Castle also has to be placed in a social context that was being transformed by other cultural movements too, namely the Renaissance and the Reformation. The latter was to have a particular impact on Ireland, as the country did not follow the general European experience of *cuius regio eius religio*, where the people followed the confessional tendencies of their rulers. Instead, the vast bulk of the Gaelic-Irish and Anglo-Irish population remained Catholic, while their monarchy went on to embrace Protestantism.

The chief aristocrat in Munster, the earl of Desmond, in an attempt to protect medieval privileges, rebelled against the ambitious reforms of the Protestant Tudor state. The rebellion resulted in large areas across Munster being devastated by war and depopulation. Estates belonging to the earl and his followers, comprising an estimated 480,000 acres, were confiscated in 1584. Subsequently, these escheated lands was ratified by an act of parliament in Dublin in 1585–6, paving the way for a new colony or plantation of English settlers, though this time Protestant in affiliation.[31] Given the Reformation, there were serious tensions between England and Spain, with concerns over a potential conquest of Ireland, and the island being used as a means to invade England. These strategic considerations, combined with increasing animosity to the Catholic faith, meant that the notion of establishing new English colonies in Ireland became popular. At the same time, the older conciliatory policies towards the native elite did not altogether disappear as the lordship of Muskerry was granted to Sir Cormac mac Taidhg by royal patent in 1578.[32] During the course of the Desmond Rebellion, James Sussex Fitzgerald, a leading rebel and brother to the earl, was captured by the MacCarthys of Carrignamuck Castle during an attempted cattle raid into Muskerry. Sir Cormac ordered his confinement in Carrigadrohid Castle, where he was soon after surrendered to Sir Warham St Leger, an English army officer, who duly executed him for treason.[33] After the death of Sir Cormac in 1583, the title passed to his brother Ceallachán mac Taidhg, who was persuaded in the following year to stand aside in favour of a nephew, Sir Cormac Óg mac Diarmada.[34]

In 1588, Sir Cormac mac Diarmada attended parliament as the baron of Blarney, and in the following year surrendered his lands to the crown. He obtained a regrant in the process, going through the same procedures as his uncle, Sir Cormac mac Taidhg, a decade beforehand.[35] Cormac mac Diarmada faced a challenging time in his tenure as lord of Muskerry. The end of the century saw the outbreak of the Nine Years War (1594–1603), when the bulk of the native aristocracy came together under the leadership of Hugh O'Neill, earl of Tyrone, in open defiance of the English crown. This conflict was the closest that the English ever came to being forced out of Ireland, with well equipped armies facing each other as well as widespread guerrilla warfare across the country. Cormac mac Diarmada attempted to navigate a middle course, placating both the crown administration and the resurgent native rebels. On 13 May 1601, from 'my house of Blarney', Cormac mac Diarmada wrote to Sir Robert Cecil

1.5 During the course of the Nine Years War (1594–1603), the coastal town of Kinsale was held by a Spanish expeditionary force in the autumn and winter of 1601, and consequently besieged by the English army, who in turn were encircled by the Irish forces of Hugh O'Neill, earl of Tyrone, and Red Hugh O'Donnell, earl of Tyrconnell. English efforts to break the stalemate resulted in the routing of the Irish and the surrender of the Spanish (image from *Pacata Hibernia*).

3: The Battle of Kinsale

In the early 1590s, a rebellion in the north of Ireland escalated into an island-wide conflict, subsequently referred to as the Nine Years War (1594–1603). This war, led by one of the chief noblemen in Ulster, Hugh O'Neill, the earl of Tyrone, nearly saw the end of English rule in the country. Irish lords feared that their rights and privileges under the old customs and traditions of Gaelic Ireland would be lost if Elizabethan reforms went unchallenged. From an English perspective, Protestant England was at that time pitched against the powerful Catholic kingdoms of France and Spain, and there were fears that a rebellious Ireland could be used by these continental powers as a base from which to launch an invasion of England. These concerns were realized when a Spanish expeditionary force of 4,000 infantry under Don Juan del Águila landed at the southern port of Kinsale, Co. Cork, on 21 September 1601. A standoff ensued, with the Spanish surrounded by the English forces of Charles Blount, Lord Mountjoy, who in turn were encircled by the Irish, led by the earl of Tyrone and Red Hugh O'Donnell, earl of Tyrconnell. On 25 December, in an effort to break the stalemate, the English broke out from their positions and attacked the Irish. The battle was over within a few hours, with the Irish completely routed. The Spanish stayed within their defences, preferring to keep out of the battle, and left the field to the victorious English. They surrendered to Lord Mountjoy's forces nine days later, and departed from Ireland the following March under terms. The Battle of Kinsale was a turning point in the war, with the earl of Tyrone eventually suing for peace with the Treaty of Mellifont in 1603.

1.6 Kilcrea friary, a Franciscan foundation, was also established by Cormac 'Láidir' mac Taidhg MacCarthy, the famed builder of Blarney Castle. In medieval times, it was quite common for the Gaelic lords to patronize monastic communities – the Franciscans being a popular choice due to their strong pastoral mission. The church in the monastery is marked by a belfry, with other well-preserved buildings arranged around a cloister.

(one of Queen Elizabeth's closest advisors), demonstrating his loyalty with an account of how he had refused to join the rebel earl of Tyrone, how he had sent the heads of rebels slain by him to the president of Munster (the monarch's chief representative in the region), and how he was wounded in the service of the crown, losing many of his gentlemen and followers in the process.[36] Yet, a few months later, on 7 December 1601, the Anglo-Irish earl of Ormond informed Cecil that when Tyrone had arrived in Muskerry, Cormac's kinsmen and followers had joined in the rebellion.[37]

The Battle of Kinsale in 1601 was a critical juncture in the war, the result of which saw a reversal of fortune for the rebels. English forces managed to successfully besiege a Spanish expeditionary force that had landed at Kinsale, while staving off and putting flight to an attack by the earl of Tyrone. A near contemporary account, the *Pacata Hibernia*, described the run of the battle, with the lord deputy of the time, Lord Mountjoy, ordering Cormac mac Diarmada to march his men by the Spanish trenches, to prove that Irish support lay with the English.[38] The aftermath of the Battle of Kinsale saw further reversals of fortune for the earl of Tyrone and his followers, who were eventually brought to heal by 1603. The subsequent mass confiscation of lands in the north of Ireland was to clear the way for a new programme of settlement by Protestant English and Scottish settlers there. In 1607,

1.7 Even after the dissolution of monasteries in the sixteenth century, church sites continued to be used as burial places, particularly by the descendants of the original founding benefactor. The arched wall niche in the north-east corner of the altar at Kilcrea friary is reputed to be the ancestral tomb of the Muskerry MacCarthys. Cormac Óg mac Diarmada MacCarthy (d. 1616) was the last lord of Muskerry to be interred there.

under fear of arrest and confiscation, Hugh O'Neill, the earl of Tyrone, along with his strongest cohorts, Rory O'Donnell, the earl of Tyrconnell and Cuconnaught Maguire of Fermanagh, fled to the continent. Known by historians since as the 'Flight of the Earls', this single event encapsulated the decline of Gaelic Ireland as an independent entity and cleared the way for the establishment of the Ulster Plantation, which saw large numbers of British settlers move into the north of the country.

The perceived ambivalence of Sir Cormac mac Diarmada during the Nine Years War may have allowed the name 'Blarney' to pass into modern parlance both as a noun referring to smoothly flattering and cajoling talk, as well as a verb to overcome or beguile with flattery.[39] The astute manoeuvrings of Cormac mac Diarmada may also have given rise to the legend that a stone embedded in the battlements bequeathed the power of compelling speech to those who kissed it.[40] By the early decades of the nineteenth century, this legend was already in vogue, as

> a stone in the highest part of the castle wall is pointed out to visitors, which is supposed to give to whoever kisses it the peculiar knowledge of deviating from veracity with unblushing countenance whenever it may be convenient – hence the well-known phrase of 'Blarney'.[41]

This tradition was further popularized in the nineteenth century by the Jesuit priest Francis Sylvester Mahony, who published under the pseudonym Father Prout a song-poem in his *Reliques* of 1860:

> There is a stone there
> That whoever kisses
> Oh! he never misses
> To grow eloquent ... [42]

The MacCarthys as landlords in the English fashion

Despite being eventually arrested in the aftermath of the Battle of Kinsale on suspicion of complicity with the rebels, Cormac mac Diarmada was pardoned and allowed to return to his estates, holding the same until his death in Blarney Castle in February 1616.[43] His remains were interred in the ancestral tomb at the Franciscan friary in Kilcrea, apparently the last lord of Muskerry to be buried there (figs 1.6 & 1.7).[44] The native aristocracy who still held substantial estates in the early seventeenth century sought to maintain their political and social standing in a society that was becoming increasingly anglicized with the arrival of more and more settlers from Britain, and not just in Ulster. In Munster, the years between 1603 and 1622 saw a renewed influx of settlers, reaching a peak in 1622 with a good deal of continuity in ownership and in the pattern of development from before the turmoil of the Nine Years War.[45] Occasional comments in 1622 noted 'the continual increase of plantations' in Munster; and that the settlers there 'are much increased and the country doth begin to grow full of English'.[46] In these circumstances, the lords of Muskerry needed to redefine and present themselves as landlords in the English tradition given the expansive agenda of the colonial order. Contrary to the native laws of succession, Cormac mac Diarmada was succeeded by his son, Cormac Óg mac Cormaic Óig of Kilcrea, who obtained his father's lands at Blarney, which were surrendered and re-granted to him in 1618.[47] This MacCarthy lord was created Viscount Muskerry and Baron of Blarney in 1628, testimony to the now pervasive influence of English political and cultural norms.[48] The expansion of central government across Ireland with officials such as sheriffs and justices of the peace responsible for local administration, pruned the ambitions of the landed elite. Also the structures of landownership were being transformed with various grades of leaseholders coming to own properties in their own right according to the norms of English common law. Many of the lordly exactions such as providing food and labour services to the local lord were transmuted into the monetary equivalents of rents and taxes, much of which now went into government coffers to pay for the emergent county administrations. In addition, the route to power presently lay in service to the crown or influence with the administration in Dublin Castle. Both Cormac mac

1.8 Contemporary illustration of a massacre of English settlers by Irish rebels. In October 1641, an uprising broke out in Ulster and within months spread across the rest of the country. Attacks against settlers, their families and property became widespread, as the Catholic population sought to regain lands and status that had been lost in previous decades through confiscation, plantation and declining economic fortunes.

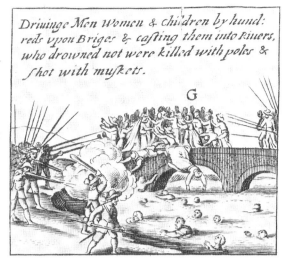

*Driuinge Men Women & children by hund:
reds vpon Briges & casting them into Riuers,
who drowned not were killed with poles &
shot with muskets.*

G

Diarmada and Cormac Óg would have understood this and pursued their ambitions in the appropriate manner.

Yet, religion was to complicate matters as a clash of interest was inevitable between a government that demanded adherence to the Protestant faith as proof of loyalty to the state and a population that remained steadfastly attached to the Catholic faith. In the seventeenth century, religion was not considered solely a matter of private conscience and Catholics somehow had to square loyalty to the Vatican with loyalty to the English monarchy. Through the 1620s and 1630s, there were demands for Catholics to be allowed to enter the army and government as well as for their property rights to be respected and safeguarded. In England, there were increasing tensions between the monarchy and the parliament, the latter concerned at the rule of the former, particularly in matters of taxation and religious conformity. Fears in Ireland of a parliament in London dominated by English Protestant radicals were accentuated by broken promises made by the crown to alleviate repressive laws against Catholics. This convinced many that rebellion was the only alternative left open to them. In October 1641, rebellion broke out in Ulster once again and duly spread to the rest of the country within months. Attacks against settlers, their families and property became widespread (fig. 1.8). By October 1642, the Gaelic and Anglo-Irish aristocracy, along with the support of the Roman Catholic hierarchy, came together to establish the Catholic Confederation. This body of Ireland's Catholic elite established a national assembly supported by a system of provincial and county assemblies. In the meantime, civil war in England had erupted, seriously compromising English efforts to control the situation in Ireland. Cormac Óg had already being succeeded by his son Donnchadh mac Cormaic Óig in 1640,[49] and it was this particular Lord Muskerry who became a leading light in Confederate forces during the troubles of 1641–53. In April 1642, the MacCarthys encamped at

Rochfordstown, south-west of Cork city, but a surprise attack by the parliamentarian garrison in Cork broke through and dispersed their forces.[50] Subsequently, in August, every MacCarthy landowner in Cork was indicted for treason and declared outlaws by a court established by the earl of Cork, Richard Boyle, in Youghal.[51] Unlike in previous conflicts, Blarney Castle did not remain impregnable, and in 1646 the tower house was eventually taken by parliamentary forces led by Lord Broghill, a son of the said earl of Cork. Yet, the castles at Kilcrea, Carrigadrohid and Macroom, all in Co. Cork, were to remain in Donnchadh MacCarthy's hands until 1650 and it appears that the latter castle served as the main residence at this time, for it was here that Giovanni Battista Rinuccini, the papal legate, was entertained for a week in 1645.[52]

This conflict in Ireland saw different forces vying for pre-eminence – Catholic and Protestant, royalist and parliamentarian – a war in which no single interest group could overcome the other. This was to change with the cessation of the English Civil War and the execution of Charles I in 1649. This freed parliament to dispatch one of the largest armies ever sent to Ireland under the command of Oliver Cromwell. The presence of a professional army under an experienced general saw the balance tilt in favour of Protestants who supported parliament. Within months, Catholic resistance began to fold; with the port towns of Drogheda and Wexford feeling the full brunt of Cromwell's zeal. Sieges there were concluded in a bloody manner. Despite this, Donnchadh was to continue in the Catholic cause, becoming one of the last commanders to finally surrender to the Cromwellian army under General Ludlow at Ross Castle near Killarney in 1652.[53] Shortly afterwards, a survey established by a victorious parliamentarian administration, described Blarney Castle in 1654 in the following manner:

> on ye prmisses is ye Castle of Blarny vald at £200 with a bawn and gardn within a stone wall about 4 acres of land, & also a new stone house, & stable, slated with a gatehouse & severall small cabbins etc.[54]

The Blarney estate was recorded in this survey to facilitate its confiscation, a fate met by most Catholic landowners in the aftermath of the Cromwellian reconquest. Blarney Castle was granted to Lord Broghill, not an unlikely outcome as he was one of the leading figures in the local Protestant gentry. Lord Muskerry was tried as a war criminal but acquitted and exiled to the Continent where he eventually joined the Stuart court in France.[55] It was during this period of exile in Louis XIV's Paris, that Lord Muskerry's wife apparently in response to a servant urging her to hasten to the window to view the 'Sun King' returning from a victorious engagement, retorted 'I have seen MacCarthy entering Blarney and what can Paris offer to equal that?'[56] In reward for his loyalty to the royalist cause, Donnchadh was created earl of Clancarty in 1658, and after the return of Charles II to the English throne, the earl and his son Charles, Viscount Muskerry, were restored to the greater part of their estates in 1661/2.[57] Ironically, it was the earl of Orrery, formerly Lord Broghill, who had taken

Blarney Castle out of MacCarthy hands in the late troubles, who introduced the bill into the Dublin parliament to have the entire estate restored, informing the Duke of Ormond (then lord lieutenant of Ireland and prime mover behind the effort), that the support of most members had been assured.[58] However, the Earl Clancarty was not to enjoy his recovered wealth for too long as he passed away in London in August 1665. His son, the Viscount Muskerry, had pre-deceased him by just over a month in a naval engagement against the Dutch off the English coast at Harwich.[59] He was buried with honours at Westminster Abbey.[60] According to the terms of a will, 'the manor-house and castle of Blarney' were passed on to his wife Helen Butler.[61] Donnchadh was succeeded only for a short while by his young grandson, Charles James, until he too died at the tender age of about 3 in September 1666. The title and lands then passed to another son of Donnchadh's, Callaghan, who had entered seminary life in France some years before. Yet he had not been ordained by this stage, and subsequently married Elizabeth Fitzgerald, daughter of the late earl of Kildare. Elizabeth, a Protestant, was outraged to find out that Dublin gossip alleged her to have married an ordained Catholic priest![62] The latter couple's only son, called Donough mac Callaghan, became the fourth earl of Clancarty in 1676.[63] The MacCarthys at this stage still held vast lands including a number of residences, and it has been suggested that the main abode for the earls Clancarty was not now at Blarney but at Macroom Castle, further west up the Lee valley.[64] Indeed, Blarney Castle may have had a new resident altogether, the Revd Roland Davies, appointed as rector to the local parish of Garrycloyne in 1681. The Anglican clergyman resided in Blarney Castle as a tenant of Lady MacCarthy, and the Davies' family genealogy records the births of the dean's children there in 1682, 1683 and 1685.[65]

While nominally a Protestant, Donough mac Callaghan, the fourth earl of Clancarty, publicly embraced the Catholic faith in the reign of James II. He rallied to the latter's cause in the Glorious Revolution (or the Williamite War as it is known in Ireland) of 1689–91.[66] The earl of Clancarty, along with other local lords, welcomed James II on his landing at Kinsale in 1689.[67] The earl accompanied the king to Dublin and though still a minor, sat in the House of Lords.[68] The outbreak of hostilities again in Ireland made it imperative for the Revd Davies to take up temporary residence in England, especially as the castle was used to imprison Protestants.[69] The earl himself saw action at the siege of Derry and on one occasion is reputed to have nearly breached the walls at the 'Butcher's Gate'. He was also involved in the defence of Elizabeth Fort in Cork city and was taken prisoner there when the city surrendered in 1690.[70] The earl was transported to London and confined in the Tower of London, only to eventually escape in 1694 from there and make his way to France, where he was given an officer's command by the exiled King James. In 1697, he paid a visit to his wife still in England, where he was arrested yet again.[71] Back in Ireland, Roland Davies returned to Blarney, though only for a short period, as the Muskerry estates were again confiscated.[72] Given the earl's connections and the fact that King William regarded him as 'that little spark Lord Clancarty', the doughty aristocrat was granted

1.9 Eighteenth-century portrait reputed to be that of George Charles Jefferyes, son of James St John. He and his wife, Anne La Touche, may have been responsible for a number of alterations made to Blarney Castle, particularly the insertion of the larger windows and the blocking of the classical fireplace in the 'Great Hall' (photograph by Margaret Lantry, courtesy of the Blarney Castle Estate).

4: The later owners of Blarney Castle

After Blarney was confiscated from the MacCarthys in the aftermath of the Williamite War (1689–91), the castle was eventually sold to Sir James Jefferyes in 1703, a military career officer and governor of the city of Cork. His grandson, James St John Jefferyes, developed the estate substantially in the mid-eighteenth century, building a Georgian-Gothic mansion on the site of the earlier MacCarthy manor house located beside the castle. At the same time, the village of Blarney was laid out with a new square as its focus, around which cottagers and tenants could live. Economic development on the estate was also encouraged, with a number of mills established in the village, including a linen mill. Following the burning of the Gothic-Georgian mansion in 1820, the Jefferyeses left Blarney and moved to east Cork, though they kept the village and surrounding lands in their ownership. The estate eventually passed into the ownership of the Colthurst family on the marriage of Louisa Jane Jefferyes to Sir George Conway Colthurst in January 1846. The Colthursts were already well settled in Ireland by this stage: one ancestor, John Colthurst, was allegedly killed in an Irish attack in 1607, while another, Christopher, was killed near Macroom in the 1641 uprising. Despite such setbacks, the family went on to establish themselves as prominent members of the Protestant gentry in Co. Cork during the course of the eighteenth and nineteenth centuries (Mosley (ed.), *Burke's peerage*, i, pp 633–4).

a royal pardon on condition of removing himself to permanent exile abroad. The earl thereafter established himself on an island on the River Elbe near the German city of Hamburg, where he resided until his death in 1734.[73] The ending of hostilities, further confiscations and the implementation of repressive penal laws against Catholics brought the final demise of the old Catholic aristocracy. The seventeenth century witnessed revolutionary changes in the structure of landownership in Ireland. In 1610, about 2,000 Catholic gentry held most of the land; by 1641 they still held 59 per cent; in 1660 only 22 per cent; and by 1703 as little as 14 per cent. Such a trend was catastrophic for the Catholic community and established the basis for the Protestant Ascendancy, which dominated Ireland in the following century.[74]

Blarney Castle in modern times

Blarney Castle was purchased by the Hollow Sword Blade Company, evicting Davies,[75] who remained as rector in the parish even after his appointment as dean of Cork in 1709.[76] This company thereafter sold 'the village, castle, mills, fairs, customs and all the lands and the park thereto belonging, containing 1401 acres' to the lord chief justice, Sir Richard Pyne, in 1702. He quickly sold his interest the following year to Sir James Jefferyes, governor of the city of Cork, who, prior to the revolution, was a high-ranking officer in an infantry regiment in Sweden.[77] He obtained for his eldest son James in 1701 the post of secretary to the British envoy at Stockholm.[78] In the course of his diplomatic duties, Captain James Jefferyes (he had obtained an army commission in 1706) was the only British officer who attended Charles XII of Sweden in his campaigns of 1708 and 1709 against the Russians, including the Battle of Pultawa, where he was taken prisoner. He was eventually released and made his way to London nearly a year later.[79] Captain Jefferyes went on to pursue his diplomatic career in both the Swedish and Russian courts, paying only brief visits to Blarney, which he inherited on Sir James' death in 1722.[80]

After the turmoil of the previous century, the eighteenth century was marked by relative stability. The descendants of the various English families who had first come to Ireland in the 1600s could now enjoy their status as the landed elite, becoming known as the Protestant Ascendancy (fig. 1.9). Many country estates were now being laid out with fine country houses (typically Georgian in style) surrounded by demesne parkland similar to what can be seen at Blarney today. The neo-Gothic mansion built to the east of the tower house may have been built by Sir James Jefferyes soon after he purchased the property,[81] though judging by the obvious Georgian influence in its design, it is more likely to have been constructed at some stage closer to the mid-eighteenth century. This house, finely depicted by Gabriel Beranger in a drawing of *c.*1775–7, is considered to be the earliest appearance of neo-Gothic architecture in Ireland (fig. 1.10).[82] This four-storey residence was graced with a central bow crowned with a crenellated turret. The fenestration consisted of

1.10 Gabriel Beranger's late eighteenth-century drawing of the Georgian-Gothic mansion erected beside Blarney Castle; a four-storey residence with a central bow crowned with a crenellated turret. The front elevation was graced with pointed windows, with the parapet level topped with curvilinear pinnacled battlements. The building is considered to be the earliest appearance of neo-Gothic architecture in Ireland (image by permission of the Royal Irish Academy © RIA).

pointed windows, with the parapet level topped with curvilinear pinnacled battlements. Charles Smith in his *Ancient and present state of the county and city of Cork*, originally published in 1750, described the gardens of the castle as being 'well laid out and kept in good order'.[83] The same family also laid out a landscape garden known as the 'Rock Close', where stones were arranged to look as if they were prehistoric megalithic tombs (fig. 1.11). In 1776, St John Jefferyes was noted as having improved Blarney Castle and its environs, forming an extensive pleasure garden that was laid out with considerable taste.[84] In 1797, the 'Rock Close' was described as

> a wonderful specimen of what taste & money can accomplish, whole mountains moved & piled together in happy combination the ewe & ash shooting from the hearts throw their spreadg [sic] arms across the devious wilderness'[85]

1.11 The Jefferyes family laid out extensive parklands and pleasure gardens including the 'Rock Close', where stones were arranged to create prehistoric megalithic tombs including this mock example of a portal tomb, more commonly known as a dolmen (photograph by Sara Leggett Painter).

Other features testify to a genteel life pursued by the Jefferyes; the two folly towers, the 'Keeper's Watchtower' and the 'Lookout Tower', which offered suitable retreats for family members and guests. The former is depicted by Beranger in the 1770s as flanking a single arched bridge over the River Blarney, which no longer survives (fig. 1.10). The remains of an icehouse are also to be found in the grounds of the estate, which was used for the storage of ice throughout the year.

Through the eighteenth century, many landlords developed the economic infrastructure of their estates and the surrounding area, and the Jefferyes were no exception. Captain James Jefferyes married twice. His first wife, Elizabeth Herbert, died in 1718, and he subsequently married Ann St John around 1730.[86] The latter marriage produced an heir, James St John Jefferyes, who inherited the estate on his father's death abroad in 1739.[87] The adjacent village of Blarney was formally planned and laid out as a small manufacturing centre, capitalizing on the abundant local water supply. In 1765, St John Jefferyes built a linen mill, twenty-five weavers' cottages and a bleaching green in the village, creating an industrial base to which other industries were attracted, including a bleach mill, a leather mill, a stocking factory and a tape factory.[88] By 1776, Arthur Young, the traveller and agricultural commentator, was able to say that thirteen mills had been erected by the family.[89] The town itself was built around a square and was provided with a large inn, church and market house. In the true spirit of a benevolent landlord, St John Jefferyes' ambition 'was to form a town,

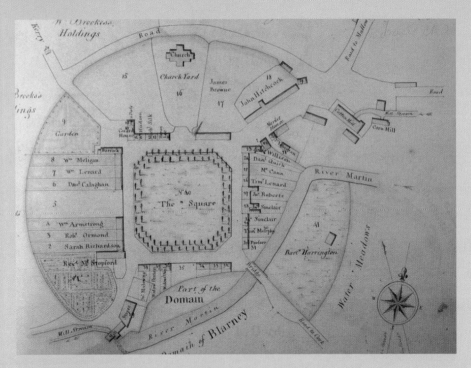

1.12 Plan of Blarney village in 1801 by David Aher. Through the eighteenth century, many landlords developed the economic infrastructure of their estates and the surrounding area, and the Jefferyeses were no exception. The adjacent village of Blarney was formally planned and laid out around a square. It was provided with an inn, a church and a market house. It was intended to create a small manufacturing centre, with various mills capitalizing on the abundant local water supply (photograph by Margaret Lantry, courtesy of the Blarney Castle Estate).

5: The village of Blarney

Most tower houses like Blarney Castle were situated on good agricultural land, with easy access to the natural resources of the area, as well as proximity to important communication routes. This encouraged the development of villages in the vicinity of these lordly residences as depicted on many maps of sixteenth- and seventeenth-century date. In 1620, Luke Gernon, an Englishman, described a settlement in neighbouring Co. Limerick as follows:

> In every village is a castle and church, but bothe in ruyne. The baser cottages are built of underwood, called wattle, and covered some w[th] thatch and some w[th] green sedge, of a round forme and w[th]out chimneys, and to my imaginacõn resemble so many hives of bees, about a country farme (from John Feehan, *Farming in Ireland* (Dublin, 2003), p. 85).

Given Blarney's status as one of the main MacCarthy strongholds in the lordship of Muskerry, it is very likely that such a village also grew in the shadow of the castle there. The political instability of the seventeenth century, however, wrought fundamental social and economic change across much of Ireland, bringing about the end of the ancient Catholic order. One consequence of this was the desertion of many rural settlements, as the traditional seats of power fell into decline, and country estates passed into the hands of new Protestant landlords. Even where settlements survived, new fashions for creating extensive parklands in the immediate vicinity of country residences meant that the cottages of tenants and other workers were moved beyond the boundaries of the demesne. This may have happened at Blarney when the Jefferyes family developed the economic infrastructure of their estate, particularly during the tenure of James St John Jefferyes, who inherited the estate in 1739. The village was planned around a new square and it developed as a small manufacturing centre. By 1765, St John Jefferyes had built a linen mill, along with a number of cottages, representing an approach taken at the time by a number of landlords who sought to develop local economies. This created an industrial base to which other firms would be attracted, including the famous Blarney Woollen Mills, established in the village during the 1850s by the O'Mahony family, and which continued to operate until the 1970s.

1.13 Pencil drawing of Blarney Castle (June 1825) from an album of sketches by S.M. Derinzy. By this time, the Gothic-Georgian house had been vacated for five years since it suffered a serious fire in 1820. Note the elaborate gothic tower sitting close to the gable-end of the residence. This tower was placed on the remains of a manor house built by the MacCarthys that had previously stood on the site in the seventeenth century (image courtesy of the Irish Architectural Archive).

to give employment to the people, and to improve the value of his estate by so doing' (fig 1.12).[90] The development of the village in the 1760s represented a new approach to encouraging an urban manufacturing base, which was to become more common in Co. Cork in the early nineteenth century.[91] Yet, economic downturns could have detrimental effects on the village, such as the recession that befell Ireland after the Napoleonic Wars. Thomas Crofton Croker recounted that

> in 1815, I remember a large square of neat cottages, and the area, a green shaded by fine old trees. Most of the cottages are now roofless; the trees have been cut down, and on my last visit, in 1821, a crop of barley was ripening in the square.[92]

1.14 The Blarney estate continued in the ownership of the Jefferyes family, until it passed through marriage to the Colthurst family in 1846. This photograph, taken in 1912, shows from left to right Richard Colthurst holding his baby daughter Mary Penelope, Sir George Colthurst, his father and then owner of Blarney Castle, and Dowager Lady Louisa Colthurst née Jefferyes, Sir George's mother (Cork City and County Archives, U196A / 2029, courtesy of Margaret Lantry).

Yet the village was to maintain an industrial base through such economic vicissitudes well into the twentieth century. The famous Blarney Woollen Mills, established in the 1850s by the O'Mahony family, continued to operate until the 1970s, and in its heyday in the 1880s employed 600 workers.[93]

The Gothic-Georgian residence itself was accidentally burnt down in 1820, resulting in the Jefferyes leaving Blarney and moving to live in Inishera House in east Cork. Quite a bit must have been saved from the mansion, considering the appearance of the following advertisement in the *Southern Reporter* of 1 November 1821:

> NOTICE – THE OLD BUILDING MATERIALS of Blarney House, adjoining the castle, to be sold at reduced PRICES; consisting of modern mahogany and deal sashes and frames, panel doors, white and black marble chimney piece and grates; a quantity of white marble flags, flooring boards, joist, ragters and slates, stone window-stools, steps and flags; kitchen range, hot-hearth and stone troughs, best liver-colour slates and large red brick; a quantity of best Irish oak of different scantlings, various other articles.

1.15 Aerial view of Blarney Castle set within verdant parkland characteristic of eighteenth- and nineteenth-century country estates. Note the Scotch-Baronial residence a couple of hundred metres to the rear of the older castle. This was constructed on the return of the Colthurst family to Blarney in 1874 (image courtesy of the Blarney Castle Estate).

In 1824, the grounds surrounding the house were described as being neglected, 'walks, which a few years since were neat and trim, are now so overrun with brambles and wild flowers as to be passed with difficulty' (fig. 1.13).[94] The Blarney estate continued though, and passed through marriage to the Colthurst family in 1846 (fig. 1.14). This family returned to Blarney in 1874 and built a new Scotch-Baronial residence a couple of hundred metres to the south-west of the tower house (fig. 1.15).[95] Towards the end of the century, American visitors disembarking from the ocean liners at Queenstown in Cork Harbour were keen to see the sights and the Blarney Stone was on many of their itineraries (fig. 1.16). It was also at this time that a light rail system was constructed to carry tourists and day-trippers to Blarney from

KISSING THE BLARNEY STONE, 4830. W.L.

1.16 Tourists visiting Blarney Castle, c.1900. The castle, with its famous stone that bequeathed 'the gift of the gab' to those that kissed it, was established from an early stage as one of the premier tourist sites in Ireland. The development of a light railway line between Cork city and Blarney brought the castle within reach of the general public, making it a popular destination. Visitors also included those who disembarked from the transatlantic liners at Queenstown (now Cobh) in Cork Harbour (Lawrence Cabinet Collection 4830; courtesy of the National Library of Ireland).

Cork city. The development of the railways in the latter half of the nineteenth century brought scenic spots like Blarney Castle and Killarney within reach of the general public and transformed them into popular vacation destinations. A reconstruction of Blarney Castle featured both in the Irish exhibition at the Olympia in London in 1888 and at the Chicago World Columbian Exposition in 1893. At the latter, the reconstruction was built at two thirds the size of the real castle.[96] Sustained emigration from Ireland to the United States and Britain ensured that sites redolent of the homeland, such as Blarney Castle, were celebrated by the Irish diaspora and their descendants. Today, the Colthursts remain in residence and manage the Blarney Castle estate, a rare example in Ireland of a country estate still being maintained to the present day.

CHAPTER 2

Irish tower houses in context

The origins and chronology of the tower house in Ireland

Blarney Castle is one of the largest examples of a type of castle known as the tower house. Such castles, typically built between the fifteenth and seventeenth centuries, are one of the most common archaeological monuments to be found across the Irish landscape. Diego Ortiz, a Spanish emissary, reported in 1567 to Philip II of Spain that 'every petty gentleman lives in a stone tower', suggesting the widespread adoption of the castellated building form by many across the social spectrum of late medieval and early modern Ireland.[1] It has been estimated that over 2,900 castles (including mottes and late fortified manor houses) were constructed in Ireland between the twelfth and seventeenth centuries, and of these, it has been recognized that the vast majority were tower houses.[2] Indeed, it has been suggested that 7,000 tower houses were constructed, a radical figure, implying that Ireland was one of the most densely castellated countries in Europe.[3] These figures are difficult to corroborate, but the massive scale of castle building as suggested does find support in mid-seventeenth-century sources, such as the Civil Survey, which record much greater numbers of castles than is evident on the Ordnance Survey maps of the early nineteenth century.[4] Studies on a regional basis also suggest a profusion of tower house architecture. Co. Limerick, in the heart of the earldom of Desmond, was peppered with over 400 castles, though it is possible that only 200 were in use by the mid-seventeenth century.[5]

In Gaelic Irish lordships, the building of tower houses in late medieval times can be seen as originating when the native polities were adopting a new attitude to their lordships. On the one hand, the Gaelic lords were diluting their claims of high kinship, but on the other, they were increasing their demands on the estates and men under their control. The presence of a tower house at the centre of such lordships provided an appropriate metaphor for the power held by the Gaelic aristocracy and gentry. These buildings, with their vertical, and in many instances hierarchical arrangement of rooms, suggest a close relationship with the social order of late medieval society.[6] While tower houses can be found in areas of the country traditionally either Gaelic Irish or Anglo-Irish, it is clear that the origin of this architectural form is to be found in the social milieu of the old colonial families in the east of the country who were accustomed to the type of built environment offered by masonry castles, and which set the stage for the daily interactions of a lordly landed household.

2.1 The vast majority of tower houses are rectilinear in plan, though a number of circular examples are known. This circular tower house at Balief Upper, Co. Kilkenny, may have been inspired by the earlier Anglo-Norman keeps of circular plan.

The origins and chronology of tower houses have been widely and often stridently debated within the last century. Thomas Westropp concluded that tower houses were mostly built in the fifteenth century, with a small number being erected in the late fourteenth, and more in the sixteenth.[7] Caoimhín Ó Danachair located the origin for Irish tower houses outside Ireland, in places like France and Spain.[8] The evidence for foreign influence is tenuous, however, with the only Irish buildings to display foreign characteristics being the fortified manor houses associated with Scottish planters in early seventeenth-century Ulster.[9] Harold Leask, a noted architectural historian, famously suggested that the origin of the tower house might be found in legislation passed by the Irish parliament in 1429.[10] This legislative act encouraged castle-building in the Pale (a region around Dublin where the English crown maintained its strongest presence) by means of a subsidy generated from a county-based levy with certain dimensions being specified for the castles (20ft by 16ft and 40ft tall). It is not clear whether this legislation stimulated the tower house

2.2 View of the late twelfth-century Anglo-Norman donjon or keep at Nenagh, Co. Tipperary, the upper portion of which is a late nineteenth-century addition. Early castles such as this would have exerted an influence on how people built castles in later centuries (© National Monuments Service: Department of Arts, Heritage and the Gaeltacht).

form, or whether tower houses already existed as appropriate models. To date, however, no castles built to these dimensions have been found and it has been suggested that the £10 subsidy would not have been enough either to encourage landowners to build, or to sway others already intent on building from altering their plans.[11]

If tower houses were already in existence by 1429, this would suggest that the origins of the tower house may lie in the fourteenth century. Unspecific references to castles or towers in fourteenth-century documentary sources have been interpreted as indicative of early tower houses.[12] Certain tower houses, such as an example at Kilteel, Co. Kildare, lacking clearly identifiable fifteenth- and sixteenth-century features, have been used to indicate a fourteenth-century provenance, though admittedly on the basis of negative evidence. Commentators see tower-house

2.3 View of the thirteenth-century hall-house protected within the walls of Glanworth Castle, Co. Cork. It has been suggested that such halls may have influenced the development of later tower houses. The division of interiors within these earlier buildings into a principle and ancillary chamber was later repeated in the floor plans of tower houses (© National Monuments Service: Department of Arts, Heritage and the Gaeltacht).

architecture as being very much influenced by fourteenth-century religious architecture, and it is unlikely, certainly in the light of the historical evidence, that no castles were built in that century either.[13] Despite this, scholars admit that there is no detailed knowledge of how tower houses would have evolved in their earliest phase of development.[14] The Anglo-Norman *donjons* or keeps of the thirteenth century may have been a source of inspiration, and these were still in use when the fashion for tower houses arose. Despite obvious differences in scale and detail, the vertical arrangement of private chambers, graded in importance from bottom to top, can be seen in both types of castles. This influence can be explicitly demonstrated in circular tower houses that are found in certain areas of Munster and south Leinster, where earlier Anglo-Norman *donjons* of circular plan can also be found (figs 2.1 & 2.2).[15] Another source of influence may be found either in the hall within larger castle complexes or the freestanding hall houses also of the thirteenth century (fig. 2.3).[16] Despite the obvious difference, with halls lacking the verticality of tower houses, the arrangement in many southern tower houses, including Blarney Castle, of a large and small chamber on each floor, may be derived from the manner in which Anglo-Norman long halls were partitioned into large and small units.[17]

Introducing tower houses as an architectural genre

Various authors have outlined the essential structure of the Irish tower house.[18] They are typically rectilinear in plan, extending four or five storeys in height, with the roofline crowned by crenellation and machicolations. The walls can be gently battered all the way to roof level, with a more pronounced base-batter as well. Despite much variation in design, the essence of tower houses is their verticality, with entrance lobby, bedrooms and hall set on top of one another instead of being laid out side-by-side as in accommodation ranges within thirteenth-century castles. A ground-floor entrance, in the form of an arched doorway with a punched surround, allows access into a lobby area. This lobby area is typically covered by a murder-hole in the ceiling above, and from this chamber one can access a small guardroom chamber flanking the entrance, a spiral stairwell to the floors above, or proceed straight ahead into a ground-floor chamber. The spiral stairwell ascends from one corner of the tower in a clockwise direction to parapet level, with each of the floors accessed via a doorway off the stairs. It is not unknown, however, for the spiral stairwell to terminate at the uppermost room and for another stairs across that room to ascend to roof level. The upper floors are usually equipped with larger, more ornate windows, fireplaces and garderobes (toilet chambers). Vaulting can support one or more of the upper floors, though in many instances there is no such feature, with wooden flooring instead used throughout the building. Windows come in a variety of shapes and sizes, but are typically flat-, round- or ogee-headed, with the larger examples divided into a number of lights with mullions and transoms. Both the internal and external wall faces of tower houses were originally rendered with a skin of harling that protected the masonry from rainwater. Such harling, being lime-based, was often white, giving rise to references in documentary sources to 'white castles of stone' and 'white-gleaming castles' (fig. 2.4).[19]

Challenges in the interpretation of tower houses

Compared to other monuments, less attention has been paid to tower houses, partly from a lack of interest on the part of archaeologists and architectural historians, and partly from the under-use of surviving physical remains and pertinent historical documentation. The apparent ubiquity of the tower house in Ireland has encouraged a rather nonchalant attitude towards it as an architectural form. Tower houses are regarded as largely unchanging, as an interlude in the typological progression between the Anglo-Norman fortresses of the twelfth and thirteenth centuries and the manor houses of the sixteenth and early seventeenth centuries. Indeed, like castle architecture in general, tower houses are often discussed in relation to how their layouts were constrained by the contradictory demands of domestic comforts and defensive realities. These approaches, however, with an emphasis on the empirical

2.4 View of restored tower house, Ballindooly Castle, Co. Galway. Its modern external rendering conveys an impression of how most tower houses would have appeared in late medieval times. These buildings were covered with a lime-based rendering called harling, typically white in colour, giving rise to references in historical sources to 'white castles of stone' or 'white-gleaming castles'. Such rendering is prone to erosion over time. As a result, the underlying wall fabric is exposed, creating the false impression among modern observers that such buildings were rather bleak in appearance.

descriptive tradition, only treat of castle forms at the very moment of their construction. Rarely is there an evaluation of how these buildings were used by the occupants or viewed by spectators in the late medieval and early modern periods.

Tom McNeill adopts a cautionary approach in interpreting the internal arrangements of Irish tower houses, noting that rooms within them may be graded and assigned functions with the same degree of confidence, or lack of it, that can be brought to bear on earlier castles in Ireland.[20] A key problem has been the lack of documentation that can be used to interpret the spatial arrangements found in a tower house. This situation has been exacerbated by the relative scarcity of surviving sources, both native and colonial, compared with those available to study contemporary English architecture. Building plans and elevations by craftsmen are unknown, while estate papers, surveys, diaries and letters that may be of relevance in illuminating the nature of life in lordly households, are either quite rare or non-existent. Building contracts between proprietors and craftsmen are also not known to have survived. Topographical depictions of buildings within their landscape settings also appear to be non-existent. There are no Irish equivalents of the English household rules composed by members of England's wealthy elite such as the earl of Huntingdon (1609) or Lord Fairfax (c.1620).[21] Furthermore, the use of contemporary travellers' accounts is limited by their inherent bias in favour of the colonial agenda, which at times translated into downright hostility against Gaelic manners, customs and traditions.[22] In *c.*1629, Geoffrey Keating, the native chronicler, criticized this tendency among English writers, asserting that from the earliest times

> Cambrensis, Spenser, Stanihurst, Hanmer, Camden, Barckly, Moryson, Davies, Campion and every other new foreigner who has written on Ireland … displayed no inclination to treat of the virtues or good qualities of the nobles among the old foreigners and the native Irish who then dwelt in Ireland.[23]

Instead, these biased writers preferred to describe the uncouthness of the very lowest orders of the people and to generalize from the vices of the few.[24] To an extent, this negative portrayal of the native lords has been somewhat ameliorated by the availability of other source material such as bardic poetry and annals.

In the absence of more detailed documentary evidence, archaeologists and architectural historians have relied heavily on the layout and features of tower houses in order to tease out some interpretation as to how these buildings functioned. This situation is further complicated by the fact that, in many instances, both the hall and other chambers are made to conform to the shape of the building, so that the difference in relative area between the hall and other private chambers is lessened.[25] Individual rooms are placed in a hierarchical ordering, where their setting is dependent on interpretations of what constitutes greater levels of domestic comfort. Larger, more ornate windows, or substantial fireplaces with carved surrounds, are taken as indicators of status. In a tower house at Clara, Co. Kilkenny, Michael Thompson, on the basis of fireplaces, identifies the principal living room as being at fourth-floor level over the vault, with further living accommodation on the second floor.[26] This is analogous to the approach taken by scholars in relation to Scottish tower houses.[27] The elevations and architectural features of a tower house express a social ordering, with the treatment of windows and doors varying according to the status of the room's expected occupants.[28] Those chambers given the most elaborate treatment are invariably those with garderobes or fireplaces. As such, the social hierarchy of a household is represented in an architectural patterning that is recognizable to the modern observer.

Late medieval architecture is linked by one common denominator, that is, its variability in form and scale. No two tower houses look exactly the same. Unlike Georgian houses, few medieval buildings replicate each other exactly. Underlying this apparent variability, however, is a common spatial ordering, linked closely to two other orders: a) the contemporary ordering of society, that is, the structuring of social and gender classes, and; b) the ordering of architectural detail and decoration.[29] Such an ordering meant that visitors to castles, perhaps of a certain status and gender, possessing certain cultural knowledge, would be equipped with an implicit

2.5 A page from the Annals of the Four Masters
(by permission of the Royal Irish Academy © RIA, MS C iii 3, fo. 218 v).

6: The annals

The annals are records of historic events year by year, such as battles and obituaries of members of the Irish nobility. There is a long tradition of keeping annals in Ireland from the early years of Christianity in the sixth century to the demise of the Gaelic-Irish order in the seventeenth century. The annals were typically written by clerical scribes in monasteries, though the practice was later continued by hereditary secular historians. Each collection reflected the interests and situation of the monastery in which they were compiled; for example the Annals of Inisfallen, which were compiled in a monastery on Lough Lene outside Killarney, Co. Kerry, covered events in Munster from the late eleventh century until 1326. One of the more famous annals are the Annals of the Four Masters (1632–6), which were compiled by the Franciscan monk Mícheál Ó Cléirigh and three associates in an attempt to collate and condense all the known annalistic material into a single source. This scholarly work took place against the decline of native political and cultural autonomy, with the arrival of new English settlers in the late sixteenth and early seventeenth century heralding profound changes in society and economy (by permission of the Royal Irish Academy © RIA, MS. C iii 3, fo. 218 v).

understanding of the spatial ordering that he or she encountered. This would allow for the appropriate mode of behaviour to be displayed: when to stop, when to turn, which areas were accessible to his or her rank, even demeanour and bodily position at each appropriate point in his or her progress through the castle.[30] This understanding of spatial organization may be likened to that of language. To read a building by the standards of social etiquette, to accord meaning to features and spaces within the tower house complex, one needed to acquire certain background knowledge, to understand the symbolism of the bawn, the hall and the parapets of the tower house. This knowledge may have been confined to certain social groups. Social identities were in part the result of performances at both mundane and ceremonial levels. Contemporaries were quite capable of making nuanced judgments about the correct modes of behaviour as evidenced in the contemporary literature. There was an element of performance in expressing such identities, with such performances being structured by the worlds in which they are set and the architecture of castles like Blarney was one way to manipulate this world.[31] This means that buildings and their surroundings were not passive entities, not merely a stage setting or arena in which people acted out their lives, but an inanimate protagonist in how social values were conveyed and reproduced.[32] As such, everyday routines in a castle household carried a 'ceremonial' significance in that they embodied values, usually implicit in that, as part of routine practice. The comings and goings of the lordly household, with their daily, seasonal and annual gatherings, served to create the castle and the identities of its inhabitants. The combination of the everyday and ceremonial, which were imbued with complex meanings and values, reinforced the social standing of the Gaelic lord. In other words, if Cormac 'Láidir' mac Taidhg built Blarney, then Blarney built Cormac 'Láidir' mac Taidhg. But such castles contained more than just the elite fixated on the communication of superior social standing. Large extended households were contained both within the castle and its immediate surroundings. Retainers and servants played an integral part in the daily workings of a lordly household, with traders, farmers and litigants also coming to the castle to pursue their business interests. Tower houses like Blarney Castle, serving the needs of a varied population, would have been interpreted in different ways regardless of what the elite consciously or unconsciously had in mind. Each visitor, according to gender or social status, would experience the castle differently. When looking at Blarney Castle today, it is important to acknowledge both the military and social attributes of the architecture, and the varied responses that it engendered.

Tower houses in the early modern era

Tower houses continued to be built in the first half of the seventeenth century in Ireland, with one of the more impressive examples being finished as late as 1643 by the O'Maddens at Derryhivenny, in Co. Galway.[33] Indeed, one architectural historian

2.6 Thomas Dineley, an English traveller in Ireland c.1680, drew twenty castles, including this example of a tower house and bawn at Ballyclogh, Co. Clare. As with Blarney Castle, a seventeenth-century manor house was built against the side of the castle, its symmetrically arranged large windows, dormered roof and chimneystacks representing a new departure in elite architecture. Note how the bawn enclosed a garden, entered through attractive gates flanked by pillars, crowned with balls or urns. The corner flankers, provided with attractive rooflines and windows, also became part of the formal garden composition (from Shirley et al. 1867, 81).

has identified the site of a tower house built as late as 1683 at Castleffrench, Co. Roscommon.[34] Of the twenty castles that Thomas Dineley, the English traveller, drew on his tours around Ireland c.1680, six were simple tower houses, still occupied at the time, while the same number possessed attached domestic wings, amply fenestrated and built against or into the older walls (fig. 2.6). Only six of Dineley's drawings show undefended houses, of which none survives.[35] In 1686, it was observed how 'several builders in Ireland have incommoded their new houses by striving to preserve some incurable or smoky castle'. Indeed, one landlord, Robert French, retained an older tower house as the centre of a symmetrical block at Monivea, Co. Galway, as late as the 1740s, while a tower house at Lohort, Co. Cork, surrounded by a bastioned bawn and moat, formed the centrepiece of a designed landscape by the early eighteenth century.[36] Thus, tower houses were an integral part of the built environment at this time, transcending the division between the late medieval and early modern periods.

CHAPTER 3

The layout and use of
Blarney Castle

Introduction

Blarney Castle, situated on a rock outcrop, in mid Co. Cork, is one of Ireland's most famous castles (fig. 3.1). In late medieval times, this was the domain of the MacCarthys, who, as lords of Muskerry, controlled much of the Lee river valley. The story of this native aristocratic family is intimately entwined with that of the tower house, a chiefry castle originally constructed in the 1480s. Gaelic-Irish lords led the way in building stone castles for their own protection, as a chiefry castle was the most likely to be attacked by rivals in attempts to dislodge the head of the family or sept from his position.[1] Unlike the large castle that can be seen today, the original tower house consisted of only a tall slender tower, four storeys in height, dominating one corner of a courtyard known as a bawn. Traces of this bawn are still visible in the north, west and south walls of the present building. The original tower survives as a block projecting from the north-west corner of the castle. At some stage in the sixteenth century, the east and south sides of this tower were greatly extended by the erection of a five-storey tower block on the site of the accompanying bawn. This development necessitated the laying out of a new bawn to the west of Blarney Castle, of which the north wall and a corner turret still survive. The endemic feuding between native elites through the sixteenth century, combined with conflicts between native and colonial interests, which enveloped Cork periodically throughout the early modern period, encouraged the continued popularity of such castellated residences (fig. 3.2).

Approaching Blarney Castle from the north through the demesne gardens, a sense of awe is created at the sight of a towering monolith perched on the edge of a rocky precipice. Its walls, built of grey limestone rubble, convey an impression of a foreboding building, dark and dank to live in. Yet, when archaeology and history are combined to recreate the past of such a place, it becomes clear that this was not simply a holdout for embattled MacCarthys, but a lordly residence in which the layout and furnishings displayed the power held by that family. Looking at the castle from the bottom of the precipice, the tower form emphasizes verticality, drawing the eye upwards. The base-batter along all sides of the building accentuates this verticality (fig. 3.3). Standing below the tower house, visitors and tenants would have

3.1 The large tower house at Blarney, constructed on the margins of the MacCarthy lordship of Muskerry, clearly demonstrated to all and sundry the economic and political strength of this Gaelic family. Endemic feuding between native elites, combined with conflicts between native and colonial interests, encouraged the continued popularity of such castellated residences through the late medieval period and beyond (image courtesy of the Blarney Castle Estate).

been able to observe various architectural features such as the crenellation, machicolation and narrow loops that allowed for the defence of the household within. While the physical appearance of Blarney Castle could articulate lordly power and authority, it was also critical in providing the backdrop for the staging of social discourse. Approaching the castle as a guest of the MacCarthy lord invoked a set of social and cultural connotations. The guest trusted the host to abide by the rules of hospitality; a need accentuated as the former came within the range of crenellated parapets and window loops. The actions of a lord reflected upon the character of the household in general. There was a collectively shared vision of ideal conduct, in which hospitality was celebrated and meanness condemned.[2]

Looking at Blarney Castle today, it is certain that the grey limestone of the walls would have been covered from view by a render or harling. Indeed, traces of this are still preserved on the exterior walls of the castle. The stone rubble was first rendered with a base coat of a rough textured lime mortar mixed with hair, fine gravel and other material, and then finished with a final skim coat of finer lime plaster bound

3.2 View of a Gaelic-Irish cattle raid in the sixteenth century from John Derrick's *The image of Irelande*, published in London in 1581 (and reproduced by John Small in Edinburgh, 1883). The raiders emerge from a forest to the left, led by a bagpipe player. To the right, a house is being set alight, and in the background a Gaelic lord on horseback oversees the removal of cattle back to the shelter of the forest.

with hair. While this rendering provided the functional role of protecting wall fabric from climatic attrition, it also played an important decorative role.[3] This paint finish, given its lime base, was typically white, hence the contemporary references to white castles. In the Annals of the Four Masters, there is an obituary to one of Blarney Castle's owners, Sir Cormac mac Taidhg who died in 1583:

> Cormac, the son of Teige, son of Cormac Oge MacCarthy, Lord of Muskerry, a comely-shaped, bright-countenanced man, who possessed most whitewashed edifices, fine-built castles, and hereditary seats of any of the descendants of Eoghan More.[4]

The appearance of whitewashed towers, sometimes on elevated sites like Blarney Castle, created a focus point in the landscape for a lordly estate. Everyone living or passing through the estate must at some stage have viewed the towering edifice. Such a view would have generated a variety of emotional responses, such as awe, respect, indifference or contempt, depending very much on the social identity and disposition of the beholder.

   The very settings of tower houses could have been used to frame natural features such as summits and waterways in an attempt to create composed surroundings. One of the chief reasons that 'watery landscapes' have gone unrecognized is that tower houses utilize sites with bodies of natural water in front or around them as is the case with Blarney Castle overlooking the junction of the Blarney and Martin rivers. Such a natural setting would not attract comment from modern researchers except if

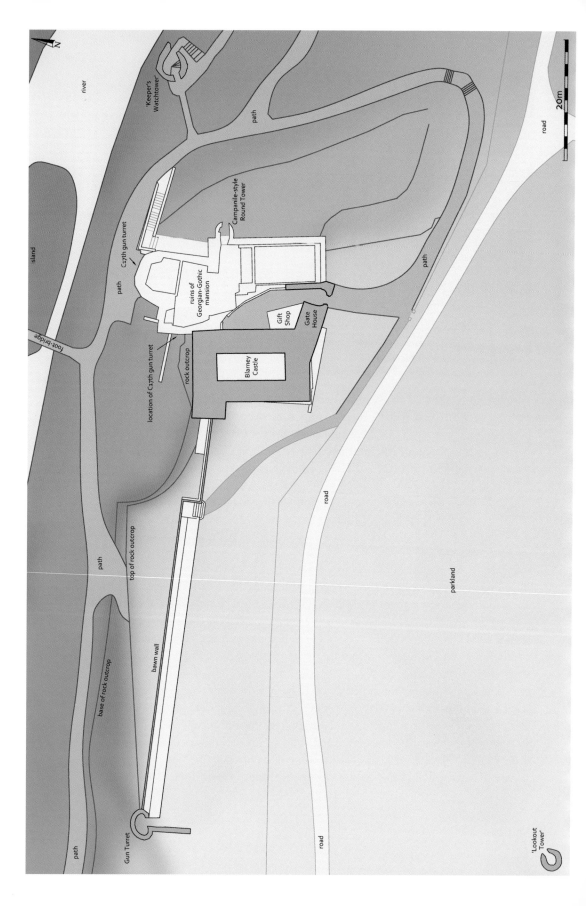

N

river

'Keeper's Watchtower'

path

Campanile-style Round Tower

C.17th gun turret

island

path

path

ruins of Georgian-Gothic mansion

foot-bridge

rock outcrop

location of C.17th gun turret

Gift Shop

Gate House

Blarney Castle

path

road

top of rock outcrop

path

parkland

bawn wall

base of rock outcrop

road

Gun Turret

road

'Lookout Tower'

20m

3.4 Little now stands of the bawn at Blarney Castle, as only the north wall remains for its complete length, albeit rebuilt in part. This bawn wall extends from the west side of the tower house to a gun turret at the north-west corner of the bawn.

medieval buildings like castles were placed in the context of other more obvious artificial landscaping.[5] The use of precipitous locations earlier had a military intent, but may have become an integral part of a composed landscape. The oriel window in the north face of the tower house at Blarney not only facilitated a vista of the surrounding estate but also acted as a feature to be seen and admired from below.

The bawn

In an era characterized by small-scale raiding and family feuding, it was necessary to provide protection for the household, servants and goods. Such protection would have come in the form of walled enclosures or courtyards known as bawns. As such, tower houses only formed a part, albeit an important one, of a greater complex surrounded by these bawns, and Blarney Castle was no exception. The operations of a large lordly estate could not be confined solely within the four walls of a tower house. The installation of byres, outhouses and kilns inside the bawn would have been necessary to provide for the demands of pastoral and arable farming, while the construction of accommodation and a kitchen house may have been required to cater for farm workers who worked in the fields of the outlaying demesne lands. A substantial hall, as well as subsidiary buildings, was revealed by excavations within

3.3 *(opposite)* Plan of Blarney Castle and its immediate environs illustrating the bawn laid out to the west of the tower house sometime in the late sixteenth or early seventeenth century. To the east, lies the remains of the Georgian-Gothic mansion built by the Jefferyes family in the mid-eighteenth century on the site of an earlier MacCarthy manor house. The 'Lookout Tower' and the 'Keeper's Watchtower' were not part of the original castle defences, but features associated with the creation of the parkland demesne that can be seen today (surveyed by Focus Surveys Ltd, prepared by Hugh Kavanagh, courtesy of the Blarney Castle Estate).

the interior of the bawn surrounding a tower house at nearby Barryscourt, home of the Barrys, an Anglo-Irish magnate family.[6] The excavation of a tower house like Barryscourt highlights the possibility that other buildings, along with gardens, accompanied Blarney Castle. Indeed, the historical sources point to this, with a bawn and garden mentioned in association with the castle in the 1650s.[7] The garden appears to have been located within the bawn itself, surrounded by 'very strong walls, and turrets with battlements and … many places of defence'.[8]

There are the remnants of two successive bawns associated with Blarney Castle, the earlier built by Cormac 'Láidir' mac Taidhg in the 1480s, only to be built over at some stage in the late sixteenth or early seventeenth century with a much larger bawn extending from the west side of the castle. Little now stands of the later bawn, as only the north wall remains for its complete length, albeit rebuilt in part. This extends from the west side of the tower house in a dog-leg fashion to an oval gun turret at the north-west corner of the bawn (fig. 3.4). A short stretch of wall footings associated with the original west wall of the bawn extends from this turret. A portion of the north bawn wall closest to the castle appears to have been rebuilt in relatively recent times, with a modern flight of steps put in place to allow access to an alure (or walkway) that runs along most of the wall length. The original wall is built of roughly coursed limestone and sandstone rubble with significant spall inclusions. Some rendering appears to have survived along the internal wall face. It appears that this defensive wall was increased substantially in width, as evidenced by the subsequent addition of a new internal wall face, with rubble infill between it and the original inner wall face. This allowed for a much wider alure along the length of the wall. Inspection indicates, however, that this new face is keyed into the north-west corner turret, in itself an original feature, suggesting that this widening was carried out at the time of the initial construction of the bawn. Clearly, the rubble core within this bawn wall meant less expenditure on masonry and mortar than would otherwise have been the case. The wall-walk was originally paved with stone flagging, as evidenced by some fragmentary remains of paving. Along this wall-walk are crenellated battlements in the form of stepped merlons with a gun ope placed centrally inside each merlon. However, abutting onto the west side of the tower house is a pair of vaults built into the precipice directly underneath the bawn wall. The function of these vaults is not clear, though they are clearly associated with post-1700 occupation of the site. A relief arch of brick and stone is evident in the internal wall face of the bawn wall above the location of the same vaults, but again its exact purpose is not known. It is pertinent to note that this portion of the bawn wall may actually be a modern insertion as an antiquarian drawing by George Holmes in the late eighteenth century illustrates that the gable end of a building was built into the angle between the castle and the bawn wall at this stage (fig. 3.5). The presence of a mullion-and-transom window indicates a late sixteenth- or early seventeenth-century date for this building, a structure that may have fulfilled a multitude of roles inside the bawn area.[9]

B L A R N E Y   C A S T L E.
Co. of Cork

3.5 A late eighteenth-century drawing of Blarney Castle by George Holmes. Such antiquarian drawings can be informative to architectural historians and archaeologists in that they may preserve aspects of a building's history that are no longer evident. In this instance, the gable end of a building is visible in the angle between the castle and the bawn wall at this stage, lit by a mullion-and-transom window, possibly seventeenth century in date (image courtesy of the National Library of Ireland).

The gun turret at the north-west corner of the bawn was designed to cover the northern and western approaches to the castle complex. This bawn was presumably defended by similar turrets at the south-west and south-east corners, given the reference in the *Pacata Hibernia* to 'four piles joined in one'.[10] The turret and bawn wall were built in a single phase. The turret is two storeys, built of roughly coursed limestone rubble (fig. 3.6). The ground floor is accessed directly from the bawn through an original brick-vaulted passage. The passage vault has been partly repaired in modern times with new brick. The first floor is directly accessed from the alure along the north bawn via a flat-headed doorway with a chamfered stone surround dressed with linear tooling typical of the early seventeenth century. The ground-floor level is equipped with five splayed and lintelled gun opes, while at first-floor level there are five similar gun opes. At some stage, this gun turret was converted into a dovecot, as five tiers of columbaria or niches were roughly inserted into the internal wall face to facilitate the nesting of pigeons. This gun turret, typically associated in the popular imagination with the grim defence of a household under siege, was modified to serve as a dovecot. The use of turrets as dovecots can be seen elsewhere, the O'Sullivan castle at Carriganass, Co. Cork, being one example.[11] Indeed, dovecots had a particular significance in England, as they were legally a prerogative of the

3.6 The gun turret at the north-west corner of the bawn was designed to cover the northern and western approaches to Blarney Castle. This bawn may also have been defended by similar turrets at the south-west and south-east corners, given the reference to 'four piles joined in one' in the *Pacata Hibernia* (written *c.*1600 but published *c.*1630). The turret and bawn wall were built in a single phase. The turret is two storeys, built of roughly coursed limestone rubble, with each floor provided with a number of gun opes. The ground floor is accessed directly from the bawn through an original brick-vaulted passage, while the first floor was accessed via the wall-walk.

manorial gentry. Such a prerogative was a direct consequence of the pigeons' tendency to feed indiscriminately on the local grain crops, and thus represented a way of converting neighbours' investment and labour into the owners' reserves of meat protein. Dovecots also provided a source of manure for the gardens.[12] In addition, these turrets could have provided an appropriate platform for viewing garden arrangements within the bawn itself. Such various uses highlight the danger of assigning definitive roles to spaces and features like gun turrets, which in reality could serve various functions, transcending perceived boundaries between the military and the domestic.

Cartographic or pictorial sources depict symmetrical garden arrangements adjacent to the residences of the landed elite such as at Macosquin, Co. Derry, where formal gardens occupied a portion of a bawn protecting a fortified residence.[13] A modern plan of Leamanagh Castle and its surroundings in the Burren, Co. Clare, depicts the remains of a formal garden with a long pond surrounded by the remnants of a substantial wall with a corner flanker surviving.[14] Thomas Dineley's drawings of gentry houses encountered during the course of an Irish tour in 1681 portray tower houses with bawns, the bawns themselves sometimes having become a garden, often entered through solid timber gates hung on handsome pillars, some of which were capped with balls or urns (fig. 2.6).[15] What is noteworthy here is that despite learned

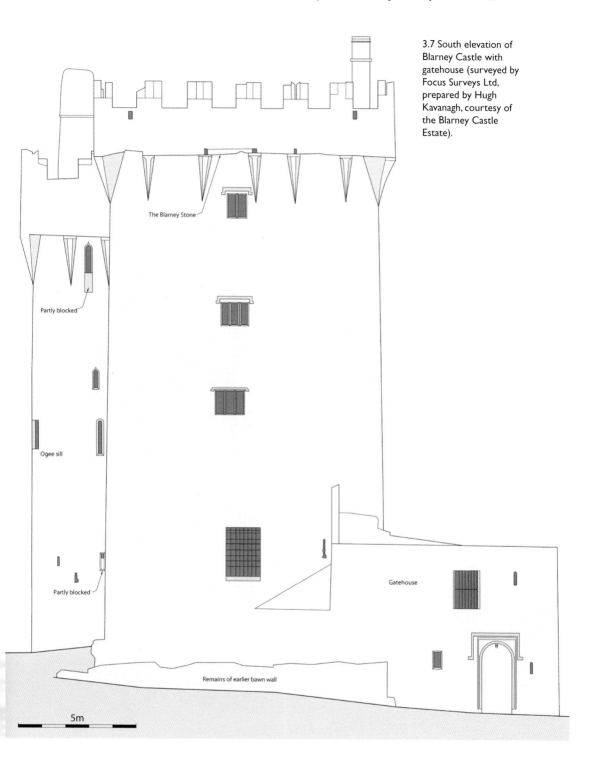

3.7 South elevation of Blarney Castle with gatehouse (surveyed by Focus Surveys Ltd, prepared by Hugh Kavanagh, courtesy of the Blarney Castle Estate).

The Blarney Stone

Partly blocked

Ogee sill

Partly blocked

Gatehouse

Remains of earlier bawn wall

5m

exhortations to transform landscapes surrounding the residences of the elite into regulated symmetrical spaces devoid of 'barbaric' naturalism, many attempts at formal gardens were restricted to the confines of walled courtyards in the shadow of castellated houses. Unfortunately, no trace of seventeenth-century garden features have survived in the vicinity of Blarney Castle, but it is important point to note that such formal gardens may be found through excavation. The interior of the bawn at Barryscourt Castle, Co. Cork, was excavated, revealing a variety of features including the remains of a garden that contained raised beds, presumably for flowers or hedging, along with a possible garden terrace.[16] At Kilcolman Castle, Co. Cork, survey and excavation failed to reveal significant features in the northern area of the bawn, suggesting to the excavator the possible presence of a walled garden, consisting of a kitchen garden on the east near service buildings and a pleasure garden on the west, overlooked by the tower house itself.[17]

The original circuit of the bawn is not known, but its layout was one to be understood from the inside out; one sees gun opes or turrets from the outside, but it was only when one stood inside the bawn, observing the comings and goings of servants, followers and retainers that one came to understand the nature of the castle's household and thus the identity of the man who was lord over it. The bawn framed the social activity within and around the castle complex. As such, the framing of architectural and social identity operated at all social levels; it was not the sole preserve of the MacCarthys and guests of their social standing. The original entrance into this bawn has not survived, but a two-storeyed gatehouse was built abutting the south-east corner of tower house, regulating the only means of access to the tower house itself.

The gatehouse

The gatehouse consists of a rectilinear building, constructed of roughly coursed limestone rubble, with well-preserved harling on the external south wall (fig. 3.8). This was built contemporaneously with the tower house, as evidenced by a passage that leads from a small chamber on the first floor of the gatehouse to a mural chamber in the south-east corner of the main building. This same passage is lit by a looped slit ope in the south wall of the tower house (fig. 3.16). Since then, further alterations have taken place, whether through the construction of the 'new stone house' in the seventeenth century, its successor the Georgian-Gothic residence in the mid-eighteenth century, or the souvenir hut to the rear in the late twentieth century. A photograph taken *c.*1870 illustrates that the front façade of the gatehouse was missing its doorway and windows (fig. 3.27). The doorway was apparently taken by an early vicar for his glebe house in the locality, but was returned at some stage before 1893. A member of the Royal Society of Antiquaries of Ireland, Arthur Hill, supervised the re-insertion of the doorway, as well as the repair of a ground-floor window.[18] Judging from the remains of the gable-end lying

3.8 (*opposite*) Access into Blarney Castle is gained through a two-storey gatehouse built against the south-east corner of the tower house. Survey of the castle indicates that the gatehouse was built contemporaneously with the tower house. Since then, further alterations have taken place. A photograph taken *c.*1870 illustrates that the front façade of the gatehouse was missing its doorway and windows. The doorway had been taken by a local vicar, who had it installed in his glebe house. In the late nineteenth century, it was retrieved and put back in place.

against the corner of the tower house, and nineteenth-century photographs, the gatehouse was two storeys in height. The fact that the first floor is covered by a vault, however, suggests that the gatehouse carried at least an extra floor, an observation given greater credence as the basal remains of a spiral stairwell is apparent at attic level in the south-east corner (fig. 3.16).

Access into the interior of the gatehouse is gained through the aforementioned doorway in the south wall (fig. 3.8). This round-arched doorway has a limestone surround, exquisitely carved and dressed in a manner that suggests a date in the seventeenth century, and is probably associated with renovations carried out to the gatehouse when a new house was built beside the castle by the MacCarthys before 1654.[19] The arch of the doorway is framed within a square hood-moulding, leaving plain spandrels. In an allusion to seventeenth-century aesthetics, a drop keystone projects from the soffit of the arch. There is a hole in the east jamb that allows a chain to pass through into the interior. This chain, when fastened from the interior, is used to keep a yett or iron grille securely in place over the door. A yett, possibly contemporary with the doorway, now blocks access when closed over the entrance. The survival of such a feature in tower houses is quite rare, with only a few examples known, such as Ballea and Cregg North, both in Co. Cork, and Clonbrock Demesne in Co. Galway.[20] This doorway allows entry into a ground-floor area that has seen significant alteration. The rear façade is largely missing and most of the ground floor is taken up with the souvenir hut, obstructing any detailed examination of the extant wall fabric. Indeed, there is no evidence for any passage or lobby area that once would have existed inside the gateway. To the right of the gateway, an embrasure for a chamfered slit ope visible in the exterior has now been blocked up and rendered over. The external surround of this window bears punch-dressing and linear tooling of early seventeenth-century date.

The first floor of the gatehouse is not accessible. This level appears to have been partitioned into a large and small chamber, the latter located inside a blocked door at the west end of the larger chamber (fig. 3.16). A flat-headed window with a cut chamfered surround in the north wall and a large flat-headed window in the south wall light the larger chamber. Beside the latter window is an original slit ope with a roughly dressed chamfered surround whose embrasure is now also blocked. This room has a segmental-headed vault, which has been partly repaired in modern times. Lit by a crude slit ope, a spiral stairwell in the south-east corner of the same room allows access to the attic level.

The tower house: ground-floor entrance

Going through the gatehouse at Blarney, visitors and members of the household would find themselves in a small courtyard with the tower house on one side and a precipice on the other (fig. 3.9). At the far end of the courtyard lies the entrance into

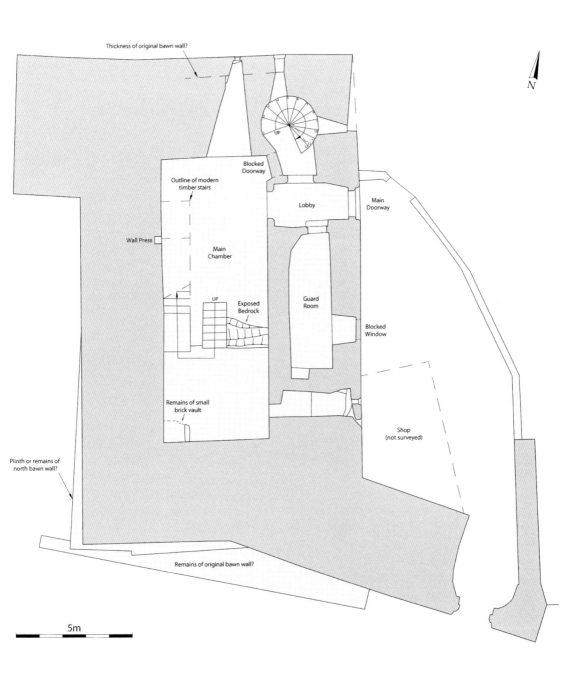

3.9 Ground-floor plan of Blarney Castle (surveyed by Hugh Kavanagh, courtesy of the Blarney Castle Estate).

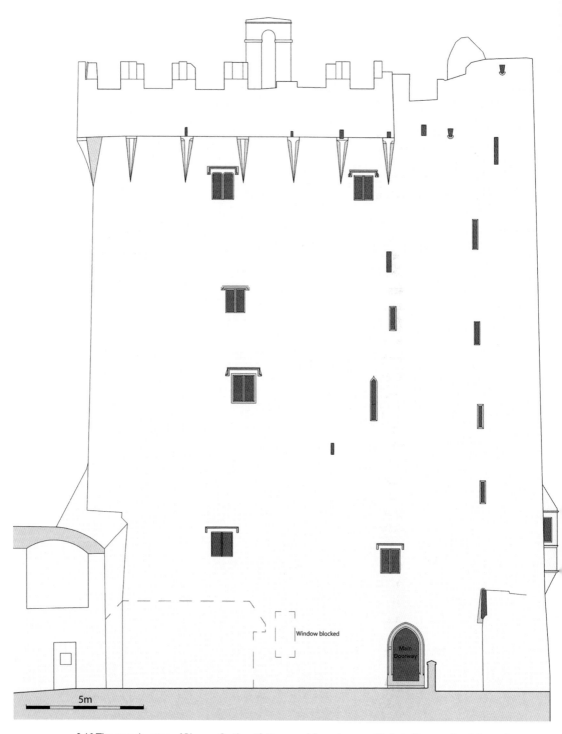

Window blocked

Main
Doorway

5m

3.10 The east elevation of Blarney Castle with its ground-floor doorway. Typical of late medieval domestic architecture is the asymmetrical arrangement of door and windows, very much at variance with the later, classically influenced buildings such as Georgian country houses, whose designs were inspired by the concepts of rationalism and harmony (surveyed by Focus Surveys Ltd, prepared by Hugh Kavanagh, courtesy of the Blarney Castle Estate).

3.11 The ground-floor entrance into the tower house at Blarney. The arched door surround is provided with a recess that originally held an iron grille or yett over the doorway. The iron hinges for such a yett are still preserved in the right-hand side of the entrance. In the opposite side is a jamb-hole that allowed a chain to pull the yett across the doorway when the occupants of the castle deemed it necessary for their security.

the tower house itself, a ground-floor doorway with a style of arch known as a double-centred arch (figs 3.10 & 3.11). Entrances to tower houses are typically located at ground level, in one of the shorter sides of the building. Their orientation tends to be eastward, though there are examples facing the other cardinal points. It is of interest that the style of doorways is quite uniform and conservative. In any given group of tower houses, the forms and sizes of windows differ, their internal planning arrangements variable to a degree, but their main entrances always possess punch-dressed and chamfered limestone surrounds, surmounted by a double-centred arch. These doorways are invariably equipped with a recess that was designed to hold an iron grille or yett over the doorway. These yetts were provided with hinges and, when

3.12 The lobby area of Blarney Castle, with its characteristic arched doorways (known by architectural specialists as double-centred doorways). The lobby itself was a transitional space where entry did not necessarily mean unhindered access to the rest of the tower house. Flanked by the guardroom and covered by the murder-hole in the vault above, visitors could still be made to feel vulnerable.

the need arose, were secured in place over the doorway by a chain that was pulled into the interior via a jamb-hole that curved through the thickness of the ground-floor wall. The iron hinges for such a yett are still preserved in the north jamb of the entrance at Blarney. It is to be presumed that the doors themselves were wooden and swung on a hinge. Such doorways are similar to those commonly found in most late medieval churches. The fact that transitional points in both secular and religious buildings were adorned with identical door surrounds touches upon one of the core dynamics of late medieval Ireland: the interdependence of lordship and church.

3.13 The lowest window visible here lights the ground-floor chamber. This window once held two lights, comparable in form and size to the windows in the more important chambers of Blarney Castle. This window is located within a portion of the castle that incorporates earlier wall fabric (the top of which is outlined by vegetation growth), possibly associated with the original bawn before it was built over with the extension of the tower house in the early sixteenth century, during the tenure of Cormac Óg Láidir mac Cormaic, ninth lord of Muskerry (1501–36). It is possible that such a large window may have originally served an ancillary hall building placed against this side of the bawn.

The lobby chamber

Passing through this entrance, one enters a vaulted lobby chamber, which allows entry into a further series of chambers: left into a guardroom; straight ahead into the principal ground-floor chamber; and right into a short ante-chamber at the base of a spiral stairwell that allows access to the floors above (fig. 3.9). All of the chambers opening off from the lobby are accessed via double-centred doorways (fig. 3.12). The lobby room itself was a liminal or transitional space where entry did not necessarily mean unhindered access to the rest of the tower house. The vulnerability of unwelcome guests was accentuated once inside the lobby, which was flanked by the guardroom and covered by the murder-hole in the vault above. Such murder-holes, typically plain rectilinear openings, can be found in many tower houses. Depending on the internal layout of the tower house, murder-holes were accessible either from the principal chamber or ancillary chamber on the first floor; in the case of Blarney Castle, from a window embrasure on the first floor. These murder-holes covered the confined space of these lobbies within a deadly range of fire, a particular advantage when assailants found themselves trapped within these confines, as all exits from the lobby chamber could be closed off.

3.14 Unusually, the southern half of the ground-floor chamber is occupied by a platform of exposed bedrock that rises c.1m in height above the floor. Sometime in the post-medieval period, this room was converted into a wine cellar with stone and brick niches built on top of this platform, against the south and east walls. Some of these still retain their brick vaulting.

Principal chamber at ground-floor level

Continuing straight through the lobby chamber, one enters the main ground-floor chamber. The shallow position of this chamber in relation to the rest of the tower house suggests a greater degree of accessibility than would be the case with the other chambers. This is a bare room with no provision for lighting except for an ogee-headed window in the north wall overlooking the precipice. Inspection of its lintel from the exterior indicates that the window originally held twin lights (fig. 3.13).[21] This poor provision for lighting can be seen as an appropriate architectural response to a chamber located at ground level, as this was the area of the building most vulnerable to attack. The sparse nature of the chamber itself also suggests a utilitarian purpose, providing a storage or service area for the apartments above. A functional interpretation for this chamber, however, solely dictated by needs of defence and security, is limited and ultimately does not allow for a more comprehensive and meaningful appreciation of how a tower house was used. The ogee-headed window in the north wall has a dressed surround and is of comparable size to windows in more elevated chambers. The use of a window similar to those lighting domestic quarters on the upper floors suggests that the ground-floor chamber at Blarney Castle could be utilized as accommodation, say for the lesser members of the household

3.15 The spiral staircase allows access to the upper floors, the newel and steps of which are finely carved and dressed, testimony to the skill of native artisans and craftsmen in the Cork region during the sixteenth century. The double-centred doorways opening off this stairwell facilitate access to the various floors of the tower house. The ascent up the stairwell created a physical and metaphorical upward movement into the very heart of the lordly residence.

such as servants, rather than solely for storage. A wall press is located in the west wall, which suggests a concern to provide for the requirements of a living space rather than simply a cellar. Wall presses are typically found in domestic spaces such as halls, withdrawing chambers and bed chambers, and were presumably used to hold household items. Whatever function this chamber served, its functionality must have been compromised somewhat by a platform of exposed bedrock that rises *c.*1m in height in the southern end of the chamber. Rough steps have been cut into the face of this bedrock platform. Sometime in the eighteenth or nineteenth century, this area

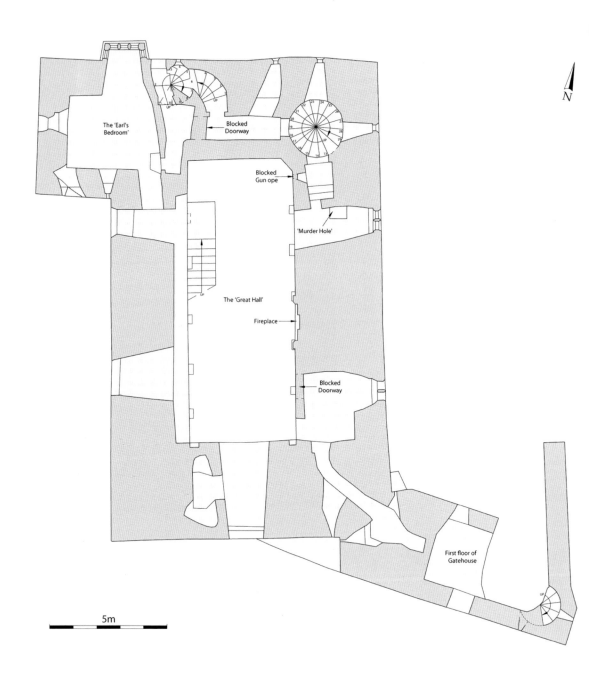

The 'Earl's Bedroom'

Blocked Doorway

Blocked Gun ope

'Murder Hole'

The 'Great Hall'

Fireplace

Blocked Doorway

First floor of Gatehouse

N

5m

3.16 First-floor plan of Blarney Castle (surveyed by Hugh Kavanagh, courtesy of the Blarney Castle Estate).

3.17 Termed the 'Great Hall', this chamber is covered with a pointed vault where plasterwork has fallen away in places, revealing the impressions of wickerwork mats. During construction of the vault, timber scaffolding was set up to support the wickerwork mats curved to the profile of the arch required. These mats held the new vault in place until the mortar had dried and the masonry had settled. Wickerwork centring was a popular construction technique in late medieval Ireland (see p. 57).

of the castle was converted into a wine cellar – on top of the rock-cut platform lie the basal remains of five or more niches of stone and brick construction arranged against the east and south walls. Two niches lying against the latter wall retain remnants of their brick vaults (fig. 3.14). From this bedrock platform, a flat-headed doorway opens in the east wall, close to the south-east corner, to allow access into a small mural chamber (a much altered embrasure serving a round-arched window as well as a gun loop set into the south-east corner). In modern times, to facilitate the large numbers of visitors, a flight of concrete steps has been built directly over the bedrock platform, followed by a flight of wooden steps placed against the west wall to allow access to the floors above.

The spiral stairwell

Originally, access to the upper floors could only be gained via the spiral stairwell that opened off the lobby area (fig. 3.9). The newel and steps of this stairwell are finely cut and dressed, testimony to the proficiency of skilled native artisans and craftsmen in the Cork region during the sixteenth century (fig. 3.15). For the most part, a flat-headed window with chamfered surround in both the north and east wall at every 360° turn lights the progress of the stairwell. Double-centred doorways with dressed surrounds opening off this stairwell facilitate access to the various floors above. The prolonged ascension up the spiral stairwell created a physical and metaphorical upward movement into the very heart of the lordly residence – the hall chamber. There was a staged progression through which glimpses of other rooms or organs of the household may have been allowed or prohibited as one made one's way clockwise up the stairwell. Such movement could create a slight sense of disorientation to the visitor who may not have been that familiar with the interior of the castle, creating a sense of discomfort before meeting the lord warming himself by his grand fireplace in the hall chamber. This progression through the interior of a tower house could invoke certain responses understood implicitly by the visitor and the household, as appropriate to the status of the visitor, whether as family member, retainer, guest or servant.

The 'Great Hall': first floor

The first doorway that the observer encounters in the progression up the stairwell is one that allows access into a short corridor built into the thickness of the east wall. The corridor terminates in a large window embrasure that has been subsequently widened to facilitate the insertion of a two-light, square hooded, mullioned window. On the floor of this embrasure is the murder-hole that covers the lobby area below. This embrasure effectively acted as an antechamber for the principal chamber at first-floor level and, once through the antechamber, visitors are confronted with a large vaulted space, known colloquially as the 'Great Hall' (fig. 3.16). The room lies underneath a pointed vault rendered with plasterwork (fig. 3.17). This plaster rendering has fallen away in parts revealing the impressions of wickerwork mats that were used in the original construction of the vault. This method of constructing vaulted ceilings was quite popular in late medieval and early modern Ireland. Timber scaffolding was erected and covered with the wickerwork mats curved to the shape of the arch required. On the surface of these wicker mats was laid a bed of mortar into which the stones of the arch were set, followed with more mortar worked in from above. Once the mortar had dried and the vault had settled quite solidly, the timber scaffolding and wickerwork centring was removed. This left impressions of the wickerwork mats in the mortar that was subsequently covered over by plaster rendering (though in many cases it appears that the wickerwork mats were left in place).

A rather fine fireplace of classical appearance has been inserted almost midway into the east wall of the 'Great Hall', necessitating the partial removal of the vault immediately above the fireplace. This flat-arched fireplace is graced with a finely cut sandstone mantle-shelf in the form of a two-tier entablature supported by consoles (also known as ancones) on either side and another console in the middle (fig. 3.19). A fireplace of similar appearance can be found in a manor house at Monkstown, Co. Cork, bearing the date 1636. Given that the construction and large-scale use of tower houses spanned a period that saw the transition between the late medieval and early modern periods, one would expect certain structural changes, such as the insertion of classically inspired fireplaces taking place within these buildings like Blarney Castle. It was at this time that the cultural norms of the elite were being transformed by notions of etiquette and social behaviour, norms very much informed by the humanist traditions of the Renaissance.

3.18 Wickerwork centring still in position on undersurface of a barrel vault at Ardamullivan Castle, Co. Galway (image courtesy of Rory Sherlock).

7: Wickerwork centring

The use of a frame made of wickerwork to support an arch during its construction was a feature of late medieval building in Ireland. In tower houses, it was common to use wicker mats to give shape to the vaults being constructed. The mats, in turn, were supported on timber scaffolding. Once the mortar had dried and the arch had set in place, the scaffolding and centring were removed, leaving the impression of the wicker mats behind. In many instances, the wicker mat was actually left attached to the vault. Any evidence for wickerwork was subsequently covered over with plaster. As tower houses fell into ruin, the ceiling plaster gradually fell away, exposing the original wickerwork on the surface of the vaults. This building technique was to survive into the first half of the seventeenth century, with Irish masons building manor houses for English and Irish landlords. A French traveller, Bouillaye le Gouz, wrote in 1644 that 'many of them [the Irish nobility] ornament their ceilings with branches' (Leask, *Irish castles*, p. 91). The use of branches to adorn their ceilings may have alluded to vaulted ceilings where wattle centring had been left in place exposed to the viewer.

3.19 While no household documents survive from the tenure of the MacCarthys, the 'Great Hall', as it was termed by the Victorians, was certainly an important room by the early seventeenth century, judging from the ornate fireplace that was inserted into the east wall. This flat-arched fireplace bears a finely carved sandstone mantle-shelf with a two-tier entablature supported by consoles (also known as ancones) on either side, and another console in the middle. A fireplace of similar appearance, bearing the date 1636, can be found in a manor house at Monkstown, Co. Cork.

The earliest surviving classical fireplace in Ireland, dating from 1565, is to be found in the gallery of Ormond Castle at Carrick-on-Suir, built for 'Black Tom', the tenth earl of Ormond.[22] In spite of such an early example, however, classicism only made a limited impact in the sixteenth century, and it was only after the conclusion of the Nine Years War in 1603 that classicism began to spread in Ireland.[23] While the incentive to adopt classicism stemmed from the migration of British settlers into the country, there is considerable evidence that a variety of native Irishmen, including the MacCarthys, developed a taste for the medium of classical art. One of the motivating factors for this may have been the Counter-Reformation in Ireland.[24] The sons of the Gaelic Irish landed elite were sent to continental Europe to serve in religious seminaries or armies, though some sons of British settlers were also sent on the 'Grand Tour' around the European mainland. For example, the young Roger Boyle, who later became an amateur architect, travelled with his tutor to Geneva in the 1630s, where he was taught 'the knowledge of the sphere and of the architecture'.[25] His father, Richard Boyle, first earl of Cork and pre-eminent leader of the New

English Protestant community in Co. Cork, possessed a booklet with hand-drawn designs of famous monuments in perspective, which he bestowed to the earl of Arundel, a noted enthusiast, in 1628. More influential were the printed pattern books from France, Italy and the Low Countries.[26] Late medieval design, however, persisted in the early decades of the seventeenth century, with classical styles only embellishing certain elements of a house, such as the main entrance, fireplaces and gateways. Indeed, most residences, whether tower houses or not, appear to have eschewed classical concepts of rationalism and harmony by typically displaying façades with asymmetrical arrangements of windows, such as can be seen with Blarney Castle.[27]

The chamber on the first floor has been assigned as the Great Hall, presumably due to the presence of this rather fine fireplace. The names given to the various chambers in the tower house convey to the modern observer some intelligibility to the complex layout of rooms, connected by dark passages and stairwells. In this instance, however, nomenclature such as the 'Family Room', the 'Great Hall' or the 'Banqueting Hall' has no sound basis in existing historical sources such as household inventories. From the seventeenth century onwards, inventories became increasingly popular, describing the contents of individual rooms. No such inventory is known to have survived for Blarney Castle. The earliest mention that can be found for names like the 'Earl's Bedroom' and the 'Banqueting Hall' is to be found in Cecil Crawford Woods' article entitled 'Blarney Castle, County Cork: double structure of its keep', published in the 1896 volume of the *Journal of the Cork Historical and Archaeological Society*.[28] Crawford Woods, in a flight of fancy, accounted for the functions of the numerous chambers in the castle, describing the main chamber on the second floor as the 'drawing-room', where:

> the MacCarthy, his family and his guests spent most of their time when indoors; here they played the harp and lute, and danced and sang, and here the younger people made love, and the elders talked over the politics of the day … and in winter here they all gathered round the mighty hearth filled with blazing logs, and discussed (in Irish) such items of news as the discovery of a new world by a man named Columbus.[29]

Opening off from the 'Great Hall' are a couple of mural chambers located in the south-east and south-west corners respectively (fig. 3.16). The example in the south-east corner was originally accessed via a flat-headed doorway beside the fireplace. This doorway was blocked with rubble masonry, probably at the same time as the fireplace was inserted. A subsequent entrance was mined through the wall right beside it to allow entry into the mural chamber. This rather small room (not much bigger than a window embrasure) is lit by a square-hooded, mullioned window in the east wall, while another flat-headed doorway, this time in the south wall of the same room, allows access to a narrow passage. This passage leads, in turn, to a small

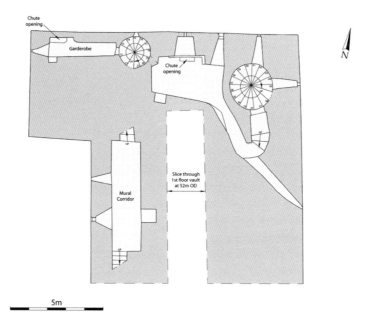

Chute
opening

Garderobe

Chute
opening

N

Slice through
1st floor vault
at 52m OD

Mural
Corridor

5m

3.20 Mezzanine level between first- and second-floor levels of Blarney Castle. It was common to have split floor levels in tower houses, with passages and smaller rooms placed within the haunches of vaults, or within the thicknesses of walls (surveyed by Hugh Kavanagh, courtesy of the Blarney Castle Estate).

chamber on the first floor of the gatehouse that abuts the south-east corner of the tower house. The second mural chamber that opens off the 'Great Hall', in the south-west corner, can be entered via the large window embrasure in the south wall. This chamber has been greatly reduced in size by the widening of the aforementioned window embrasure sometime in the eighteenth or nineteenth century. Two more embrasures serving large windows were also inserted into the west wall of the 'Great Hall' at this time; the brick-lined example closest to the north-west corner of the room allows access, via a mined through corridor, to the ground-floor chamber in the earlier tower, a chamber known as the 'Earl's Bedroom' (fig. 3.16). This route of communication between the earlier and later tower blocks is not original, and was introduced in the modern era to facilitate the large numbers of visitors to Blarney Castle each year. The insertion of the large window embrasures into the 'Great Hall' and the infilling of the classical fireplace with modern brick suggest that an attempt was made to convert this floor into a more habitable space sometime in the post-1700 era. George Charles Jefferyes (fig. 1.9) was described in 1797 as

> modernizing the domestic apartments and has enriched and added some very splendid rooms – they are in some state of progress & promise well without hurting the great original

3.21 Between first- and second-floor levels is a toilet chamber, known by castle specialists as a garderobe. The term comes from the French for wardrobe. It is reputed that ammonia discharged from human waste came back up the latrine chute and fumigated clothes stored within the chamber.

and it is to him and his wife Anne La Touche that we may possibly attribute the alterations in the 'Great Hall'.[30]

Mezzanine level between first and second floors

To proceed further up into the castle as members of the MacCarthy family, their servants and retainers would have done, one has to retrace their steps back to the spiral stairwell in the north-east corner of the building. A short number of steps up this stairwell, the visitor encounters a double-centred doorway that allows access into a mural corridor in the thickness of the north wall. This short corridor, with a roughly segmental vault, is lit by a single-light ogee-headed window with chamfered surround. At the end of the corridor, the wall has been repaired where the doorway into the earlier tower was originally located (fig. 3.16). When the tower house was being extended in the sixteenth century, it was decided to block this entrance and insert a flat-headed doorway with chamfered stone surround in the north wall of the corridor to allow access to the spiral stairwell of the earlier tower. Beyond this doorway is a short flight of steps that connects with the stairwell in the earlier tower. The steps have been mined through the wall thickness of the earlier tower and originally formed one of only two routes of communication between the two towers after the castle was extended in the sixteenth century. Why block a pre-existing entrance and go to the trouble of mining through a wall is not clear, though it could be argued that it created a greater degree of seclusion for the 'Earl's Bedroom', the chamber on the ground floor of the earlier tower.

Further up the spiral stairwell in the later extension, the observer comes upon another double-centred doorway. This allows entry into a dog-leg corridor, lit by a small flat-headed ope as it turns around the corner, via a flight of steps, towards a

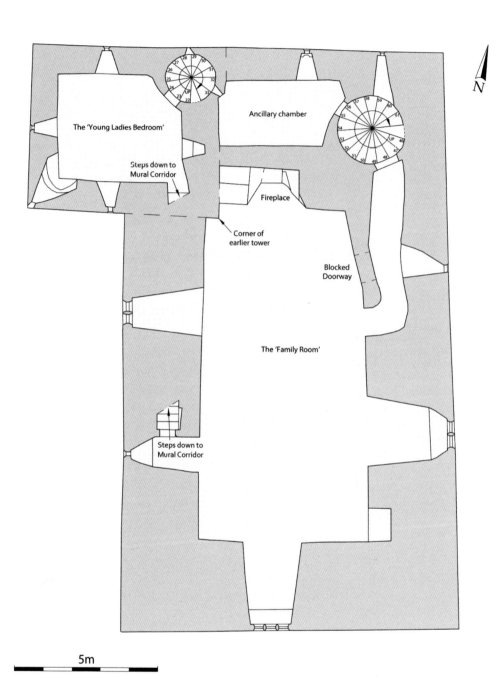

The 'Young Ladies Bedroom'

Ancillary chamber

Steps down to
Mural Corridor

Fireplace

Corner of
earlier tower

Blocked
Doorway

The 'Family Room'

Steps down to
Mural Corridor

N

5m

3.22 Second-floor plan of Blarney Castle (surveyed by Hugh Kavanagh, courtesy of the Blarney Castle Estate).

3.23 The 'Family Room' was once heated by a massive fireplace in the north wall. Its flat arch is graced with a narrow mantle-shelf. A relief arch is apparent above the mantle-shelf, though intriguingly no jambs for the fireplace are visible. This fireplace was blocked and replaced with the insertion of a narrower fireplace. The original entrance into the room was also blocked, and replaced with a brick-lined doorway. The corbels that project from the east and west walls would have carried thick wooden beams (called 'wall plates' by historic buildings specialists), which in turn supported the wooden floor for the room above.

small chamber that acted as a garderobe or toilet chamber (fig. 3.20). A number of these toilet chambers can be found in the north end of the castle, meeting the sanitary requirements of a large household. A latrine chute can be seen in the floor along the north side of the chamber, whose outlet is located in the exterior of the same wall at first-floor level. Located in the south wall at the south-west corner is a wall press. The room possesses a pointed barrel vault with traces of wicker centring. Interestingly, the corner of the earlier tower projects into this room (fig. 3.21).

The 'Family Room': second floor

The principal room on the second floor, the 'Family Room', is accessed further up the spiral stairwell via a double-centred doorway (fig. 3.22). After entering the doorway, one proceeds along a short corridor, vaulted with traces of plank centring. At the end of the corridor is an inserted brick-lined doorway, which replaced an earlier doorway just to the north of it. This allows access into a rather large room, dominated by a massive fireplace, which extends across the whole length of the north wall (fig. 3.23). Its surround consists of a joggled flat-arch graced with a narrow mantle-shelf. A relief-

3.24 In the south wall of the 'Family Room', close to the south-east corner, are the faint remains of a plaster frieze, containing spiral and floral decoration. Given the ruinous nature of most Irish tower houses, this is a rare survival of early modern plasterwork and offers an intriguing insight into the appearance of this room when in use by the lords of Muskerry. This frieze is probably contemporary with the replacement of earlier windows in the room with larger mullioned windows sometime in the late sixteenth/early seventeenth century (© National Monuments Service: Department of Arts, Heritage and the Gaeltacht).

arch is apparent above the mantle-shelf, though intriguingly no jambs for the fireplace are visible. This fireplace was blocked and infilled with the insertion of a narrower fireplace. This later fireplace bears no dressed surround, although above it, at ceiling level, is a stone cornice that extends along the full length of the north wall. A wall press with a segmental arch is located in the east wall at the south-east corner. Also in this area of the room are the fragmentary remains of a seventeenth-century plaster frieze in the south wall. Unfortunately, this frieze is rather denuded but some spiral and floral decoration appears to be in evidence (fig. 3.24). In comparison to the principal chambers below, this room seems quite spacious. One reason is that the walls of the castle on the higher floors are less substantial in thickness, greatly adding to the stability of the building (fig. 3.25). A sense of airiness was amplified by the provision of large windows in the east, south and west walls of this room, typically two- to three-light mullioned windows crowned with square hood-moulding (fig. 3.26). A couple of the mullions are nineteenth-century replacements, given their pronounced linear dressing typical of that century. A photograph of the castle taken in the 1870s clearly shows the same windows before the mullions were inserted (fig. 3.27). Yet these square-hooded windows also replaced earlier windows, as indicated by the widened embrasures for the examples in the east and south walls. In addition, visible in the external wall fabric below the windows are the stone sills of earlier single-light openings (fig. 3.28). They were in all probability ogee-headed windows similar in appearance to the existing example in the west wall.

    Windows of various sizes and forms usually punctuate the exteriors of tower houses, and the examples at Blarney Castle are no different (fig. 3.29). It is noteworthy, however, that at some stage in the late sixteenth or early seventeenth century, large square-hooded, mullioned windows were inserted. This was part of a phenomenon in which many tower houses saw improvements, with greater provision for lighting (and indeed heating, as can be seen with the inserted classical fireplace in

3.25 This longitudinal section of the later tower block illustrates how the smaller chambers were placed at split floor levels within the thickness of the castle walls. The walls of the castle on the higher floors are less substantial in thickness, improving the stability of the building (surveyed by Hugh Kavanagh, courtesy of the Blarney Castle Estate).

3.26 View of the south end of the 'Family Room' during the course of surveying the castle. The room was renovated sometime in the late sixteenth or early seventeenth century, with the insertion of larger windows, as evidenced by the widened embrasures of those in the south and east walls, the exteriors of which were decorated with square hood moulding.

Blarney Castle). As well as allowing in more light, these mullioned windows also changed perception from both within and outside the castle (fig. 3.30). On the one hand, such windows offered greater vistas of the surrounding estate, though on the other, those on the outside (tenants, visitors and passer-bys) were provided with more tantalizing glimpses of the comforts inside than would have been possible with the narrow ogee-headed windows.[31] Smaller, less ornate windows, typically flat- or round-headed slit opes, light the less important spaces such as stairwells, corridors, garderobes and ancillary chambers. The inferior status of these spaces is compounded by the fact that many of these smaller lights were rather simple affairs with no ornate surface carving or dressing.

In the side of the window embrasure serving the ogee-headed window in the west wall of the 'Family Room', there is a double-centred doorway. This doorway is graced with a chamfered punch-dressed surround bearing pyramidal chamfer stops, and allows access, via a short flight of steps, down into a mural corridor. This corridor is lit by two openings in the west wall, a chamfered ogee-headed window and a simple flat-headed opening. In the east wall, close to the south-east corner of this corridor is a flat-headed wall press with timber lintel, above which is a relief arch of brick. This

3.27 Old photographs can provide important insights into how buildings change over time. This photograph of Blarney Castle taken *c.*1870 clearly shows the windows in the south façade of the building lacking their original mullions. The gatehouse has also undergone significant renovation, with the insertion of a doorway and window into its front façade since this photograph was taken (Lawrence Cabinet Collection 1114; courtesy of the National Library of Ireland).

corridor is roofed with a vault, roughly pointed in appearance. At the far end of this passage is a flat-headed doorway of simple appearance that has been mined through the wall of the earlier tower. Three steps rise up towards this doorway which allows access into the first-floor chamber of this tower, the 'Young Ladies' Bedroom'. This is the second of the two original access points between the earlier tower of Cormac 'Láidir' mac Taidhg and the later extension (figs 3.20 & 3.22), but before proceeding into the former it is necessary to continue our progress through the larger tower block.

Mezzanine level between second and third floors

Going back up the stairwell in the north-east corner of the larger tower, with its finely carved steps and newel, a double-centred doorway allows entry directly into an ancillary chamber (fig. 3.22). This doorway has seen subsequent repair with its south jamb being completely replaced with brick. The doorway itself is located in a wall that curves to accommodate the stairwell. In addition, the corner of the stairwell block associated with the earlier tower projects into the far end of this room. A corner loop with a roughly dressed surround, which formerly lit the stairwell of the first tower, is

3.28 These square-hooded windows in the south façade of the castle replaced earlier windows. Still visible in the external wall fabric below the windows are the stone sills of earlier single-light openings. Directly above these windows, at parapet level, is the world famous Blarney Stone.

still evident in this older wall fabric (fig. 3.31). Its aperture remains unblocked, allowing occupants within this ancillary chamber a view into the stairwell as it rises through the older tower. The room is lit by a flat-headed window with a chamfered, roughly dressed surround. Underneath the sill of this window is a slop-hole that allowed for the disposal of waste water. The room possesses a pointed barrel vault, well-covered with plaster, but with traces of wickerwork centring still evident.

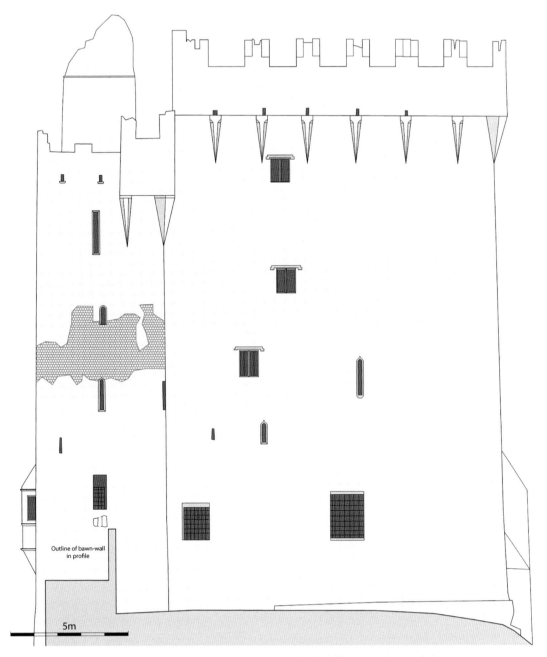

Outline of bawn-wall
in profile

5m

3.29 The west elevation of Blarney Castle. The earlier tower (to the left) was greatly extended at some stage in the early sixteenth century. Like many other tower houses in Ireland, the size and forms of the windows can vary in the one building, highlighting the social hierarchy of spaces within (survey by Focus Surveys Ltd, prepared by Hugh Kavanagh, courtesy of the Blarney Castle Estate).

3.30 Under the influence of the Renaissance, the pleasure garden with hedge-boxing and other plants laid out in symmetrical patterns was introduced into Ireland, along with the notion that the residence should form the core component of a designed landscape. At Blarney, the replacement of medieval windows with larger square-hooded, mullioned versions facilitated a greater view of such composed surroundings.

The 'Banqueting Hall': third floor

On the next floor level, opening off the stairwell is another double-centred doorway. After going through this doorway, the visitor proceeds along a short mural corridor, which is lit by a flat-headed window. This corridor opens out into the main chamber on the third floor, the 'Banqueting Hall' (fig. 3.32). The remains of a fireplace (now blocked) are located in the east wall, surmounted by a modern timber lintel. Only the finely cut chamfered jamb-stones of the fireplace surround survive (fig. 3.33). Like the 'Family Room', the room is provided with a number of square-hooded, mullioned windows, all served by rather large embrasures. These are also later insertions, as evidenced by the stone surrounds of earlier windows visible in the external wall fabric below two of these windows. Intriguingly, there is a pointed arch with traces of wicker centring projecting slightly from the north wall (fig. 3.33). Its appearance initially is rather puzzling as there is no indication on any of the other walls that this chamber was vaulted. Yet on closer inspection the shadow of the vault in the south wall (partly obscured by vegetation) is revealed, indicating that the room was indeed originally

3.31 View of ancillary chamber at mezzanine level between second and third floors. A corner of the earlier fifteenth-century tower projects into the room. Still visible in the older wall fabric is a loop that formerly lit the stairwell of the original tower.

vaulted (fig. 3.34). Indeed it is possible to follow the spring of the vault on both the east and west walls as well where the smooth wall finishing gives way to a coarser fabric. The presence of a second vault follows a pattern commonly found in Munster, where many tower houses were vaulted at both first- and third-floor levels. The fireplace, probably of comparable date to the classical fireplace below, provides a date no later than the early 1600s for the removal of the vault, as it was clearly inserted after this alteration to the castle. Subsequently, a substantial rebate along each wall supported a timber floor for the room above instead. The walls of the 'Banqueting Hall', like the walls

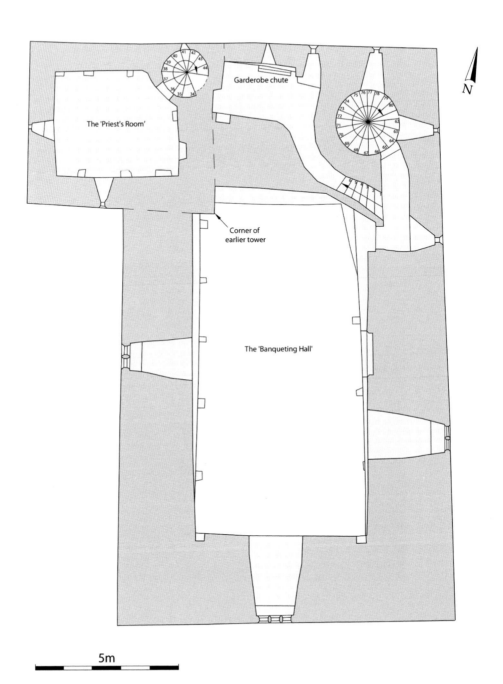

The 'Priest's Room'

Garderobe chute

Corner of
earlier tower

The 'Banqueting Hall'

N

5m

3.32 Third-floor plan of Blarney Castle (surveyed by Hugh Kavanagh, courtesy of the Blarney Castle Estate).

3.33 General view of 'Banqueting Hall' with the south-east corner of the earlier tower house evident to the left. To the right can be seen a fireplace that was subsequently inserted following the removal of a pointed vault. The stub of this vault can be clearly seen in the north wall of the room, with traces of wickerwork centring still visible (see p. 57). The presence of two vaults follows a pattern commonly encountered in Munster, where many tower houses were vaulted at both first- and third-floor levels.

throughout the rest of the castle, are rather bare, with the roughly coursed rubble masonry conveying the impression that living conditions within such spaces were uncomfortable and 'primitive' by modern standards.

Indeed, foreign contemporary accounts portray the interiors of tower houses as rather bare and poorly furnished. A French traveller, Monsieur Bouillaye le Gouz, wrote in 1644 that

> the castles of the nobility consist of four walls; extremely high and thatched with straw; but to tell the truth, they are nothing but square towers, or at least having such small apertures as to give no more light than there is in a prison. They have little furniture, and cover their rooms with rushes, of which they make their beds in summer, and straw in winter. They put the rushes a foot deep on their floors and on their windows, and many of them ornament their ceilings with branches.[32]

The use of branches to adorn their ceilings may be alluding to vaulted ceilings where wicker centring had been left in place. Such opinions do an injustice to these tower

3.34 Despite the careful removal of the vault over the 'Banqueting Hall' and the subsequent reinstatement of the wall faces, traces of the vault in the walls are outlined by vegetation growing in the coarser wall fabric.

houses, however, as these buildings provided stage settings in which guests could be received and catered for in a manner that would do service to the status of the castle owner. The status of guests governed ease of access to specific areas within the tower house, with the status of rooms communicated by scale, position, furnishings and decoration, which attested to the munificence of the owners. The best furniture, pottery and hangings were reserved for the more important chambers in the castle, serving not only the needs for domestic comfort, but also impressing upon guests the wealth and connections enjoyed by the resident family (fig. 3.35). Even if the built environment was not sophisticated by the norms of early modern Europe, Gaelic Irish families could still enjoy luxury furnishings that were more sophisticated than the physical settings in which they were placed.

The bare walls of castles like Blarney are the product of centuries of neglect and attrition, and in no way reflect their original condition. In Irish tower houses, there is clear evidence for wall finishing, with most if not all of the internal spaces, such as the halls, chambers, stairwells and passages, finished with a smooth coat of render. This render would have obscured every feature of the stone structure, including in some instances the dressed surrounds of fireplaces, doors and windows. The punch dressing evident on such dressed stone provided a key for the plasterwork. In Barryscourt Castle, Co. Cork, where render finish has recently fallen away from the walls, a pale lime-wash can be detected over the underlying rubble-stone surfaces.

3.35 Tower houses could provide comfortable accommodation for the nobility, as can be seen in the restored hall chamber in Barryscourt Castle, Co. Cork. As well as being covered with tapestries, the walls may also have been covered with decorative wooden panelling, known as wainscoting.

This was probably applied as an intermediate measure to help bind the surface before rendering. Unlike many recently 'restored' late medieval interiors in Ireland, it is unlikely that whitewashed stone rubble walls ever formed a deliberate decorative finish, even in the short term.[33] However, finished walls as well as decorative stonework did receive whitewash. Covering the interior walls with such a bright colour was a necessary device to lighten the room as much as possible. This was important in the context of rooms provided with small opes typical of tower houses.

Polychrome wall paintings are less common than in ecclesiastical contexts, but have been identified in a number of castles including four tower houses, namely Barryscourt, Co. Cork, along with Ardamullivan, Ballyportry and Urlanmore, all in the south Galway/north Clare area. In Barryscourt, the paintings are to be found in the chapel, in the north-east turret adjoining the Great Hall. The larger chambers at Ardamullivan and Ballyportry were decorated with a scheme of wall paintings, while the paintings at Urlanmore adorned an ancillary chamber at first-floor level before the castle's collapse a few years ago.[34] The lack of colour paints over wall renders in Blarney Castle does not necessarily mean that the rooms within were not painted, as such coatings can be highly sensitive to exposure and neglect. The extant

3.36 View of the principal chamber at fourth-floor level. While known as the 'Chapel', it is unlikely that this room ever specifically served a liturgical purpose. Chapels have been found in other castles, but they are usually placed in smaller, more discrete rooms, away from the public spaces like the hall. The name is presumably derived from the presence of pointed window embrasures and wall presses.

archaeological and documentary evidence, such as household inventories, points to a vigorous use of colour, achieved with the use of paint on both walls and furniture, along with colourful wall hangings such as tapestries and portraits.[35] Contemporary English inventories record that rendered walls were commonly painted in various colours, based on themes imitative of textiles, tapestry and panelling. Wooden wall panelling itself is a feature of early modern architecture in England, though it rarely survives in Ireland. An example of panelled chambers in the English West Country style survives at Myrtle Grove in Youghal, Co. Cork.[36]

Early modern bardic poetry suggests that much effort was made to furnish the interiors of tower houses. A sixteenth-century poem ascribed to Tadhg Dall Ó hUiginn claims that when Conn Ó Domhnaill and his wife Róis were occupants of Lifford Castle in Donegal, they furnished its banqueting hall with tables, cupboards and coverlets. The same poem alludes to smooth marble arches, which possibly lined the doorways or fireplaces of this great hall, acting as impressive frames for this splendidly furnished arena. A patron whose house contained luxurious and novel goods would be anxious that these find mention in praise poetry, so these furnishings probably had a basis in fact.[37] Richard Stanihurst in the 1580s described some of the furniture utilized by Gaelic Irish lords: 'At their meals, they recline, couches being supplied', but his description goes on to show that these meals were served in a large hall at ground-floor level adjoining the tower house. Yet the use of couches suggests furnished interiors.[38]

Household inventories have been invaluable in identifying the nature of furnishings in Old and New English households, however little has come to light as to how native households were furnished.[39] A rare document of native provenance survives from early modern Offaly. In his final days, the lord of Delvin Eathra, Sir John MacCoghlan, drew up his will on 10 July 1590 in the presence of witnesses in the house of Solomon MacEgan in Coole. According to the terms of his last testament, all his movable goods, corn, chattels and furniture were to be distributed among various members of his family, including dishes and pots, some of which were made of pewter. Six vessels called in English 'tonna', and two cups bought and made in the name of Sir John were specifically not to be divided up in the final distribution.[40] His epitaph in the Annals of the Four Masters records that 'There was not a man of his property, of the race of Cormac Cas, who had better furnished or more commodious courts, castles and comfortable seats, than this John'.[41] While the will does not specify individual pieces of wooden furniture, there was a range of such pieces to be found in tower houses in general. Perusal of a stray inventory detailing an Old English household in neighbouring Kilkenny suggests that the chambers of these tower houses were more than likely furnished to allow for the pursuit of a genteel lifestyle. The 1615 will of the Kilkenny merchant John Roth Fitzpiers refers to

> all the bedstedds, boordes, chairs, stooles and of all and evry uther the stuffes, furnitures and utensils of my saide house … all my diapr, holland and lynin … my tapistrie coverlet, the sey greene hangings, or curtyns of both my best bedstedds … all my drawing tables, bedsteeds, cupboords, livery cupboards, virginalls, wainscott, seelings of my hall and chambers (panelling), benchs, long-stools (forms), scabetts (stools), ioynt-stools chairs (backstools) my great cipresse chest and cipresse countor … all my pewter, brasse, batry, iron, beddings of feathers and flocks … [and] all my plate.[42]

It can be seen, therefore, that spaces within elite residences such as Blarney Castle could be furnished to a standard expected for genteel living.

Mezzanine level between third and fourth floors

A flight of stairs rises from the mural corridor to the 'Banqueting Hall' to a small mezzanine chamber located between the third- and fourth-floor levels (fig. 3.32). This room acted as a garderobe and, like the other small chambers in the north end of the sixteenth-century extension, the corner of the stairwell block associated with the earlier tower projects into this room. A latrine chute can be seen in the floor of

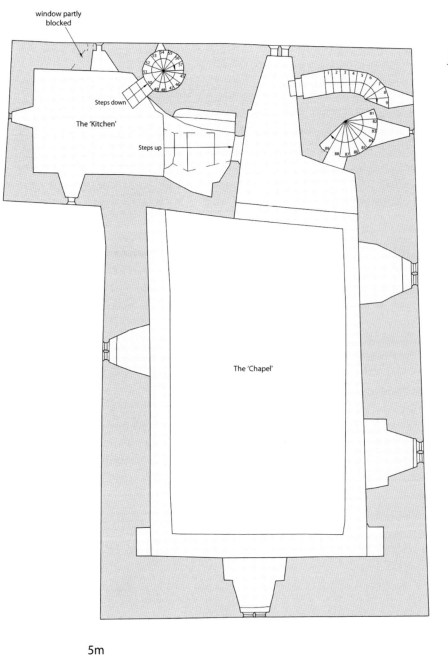

window partly
blocked

N

Steps down

The 'Kitchen'

Steps up

The 'Chapel'

5m

3.37 Fourth-floor plan of Blarney Castle. Unlike the principal chambers below, the 'Chapel' occupies the complete floor area at this level. This is characteristic of many tower houses in the south and west of Ireland, where the floor levels are divided into a principal and ancillary chamber, except for the uppermost floor. A doorway and short flight of steps were inserted to facilitate communication between the 'Kitchen' and the 'Chapel'. This route of access between the third floor of the original tower and the fourth floor of the subsequent extension was designed to facilitate the movement of visitors around the castle in modern times (surveyed by Hugh Kavanagh, courtesy of the Blarney Castle Estate).

the chamber, whose outlet is located in the north façade between the second- and third-floor levels. A slight instep and a pair of joist-holes in the north wall above this chute suggest the original presence of a latrine seat. In the south wall at another corner of the room is a wall press. This chamber is lit by two opes in the north wall, a flat-headed slit ope and a flat-headed window, both of rather basic appearance. Of interest, is a jamb-stone in the latter window that was initially prepared as the lintel for an ogee-headed window before being reused for its present purpose. Like most of the other small chambers in the castle, the room has a pointed barrel vault with traces of wicker centring.

The 'Chapel': fourth floor

The spiral stairwell finally terminates at a double-centred doorway, which allows access directly into the principal chamber at fourth-floor level, a room known as the 'Chapel', a name presumably derived from the pointed embrasures that serve the windows (fig. 3.36). Unlike the principal chambers below, the 'Chapel' occupies the complete floor area at this level (fig. 3.37). This is characteristic of many tower houses in Munster and Connacht, where the floor levels are divided into a principal and ancillary chamber except for the uppermost floor.[43] Beside the entrance to this room is a window embrasure in the north wall, one side of which contains a double-centred doorway. This second doorway, with a punch-dressed, chamfered surround with pyramidal chamfer stops, allows access to a spiral stairwell that terminates in a roof turret at parapet level. A third double-centred doorway on the other side of this window embrasure is a later insertion. This latter doorway, along with the surrounding fabric, was inserted in the eighteenth or nineteenth century to facilitate communication between the third-floor level of the late fifteenth-century tower (the 'Kitchen') and the fourth floor of the sixteenth-century extension. Two wall presses with a pointed segmental arch are located in the corners at the south end of the 'Chapel'; one of them is embellished with a chamfered arch moulding (fig. 3.36). Like the principal chambers below, this room is lit by square-hooded mullioned windows that were inserted sometime in the late sixteenth or early seventeenth century, though in the north wall the original window is still preserved – a two-light, ogee-headed window, typically fifteenth to sixteenth century (fig. 3.38).

> We are come to the castle already. The castles are built very strong, and wth narrow stayres, for security. The hall is the uppermost room, lett us go up, you shall not come downe agayne till tomorrow … The lady of the house meets you wth. her trayne … Salutations paste, you shall be presented wth. all the drinkes in the house, first the ordinary beare, then aqua vitae [whiskey], then sacke [white wine], then olde-ale, the lady tastes it, you must not refuse it. The

3.38 The 'Chapel' is lit by square-hooded mullioned windows that were inserted sometime around 1600, though in the north wall here the original window is still preserved – a two-light, ogee-headed window, typical of fifteenth- to sixteenth-century architecture, providing a picture of how the room would have appeared before the later renovations.

fyre is prepared in the middle of the hall, where you may sollace yor. selfe till supper time, you shall not want sacke and tobacco. By this time the table is spread and plentifully furnished wth. variety of meates, but ill cooked and without sauce ... When you come to yor. chamber, do not expect canopy and curtaines.[44]

Luke Gernon's 1620 description of the uppermost room in a Limerick tower house is reminiscent of many tower houses in Munster where the hall, marked by certain architectural elaboration such as a large fireplace or more ornate windows, was located on the highest floor level. The lack of documentary sources such as contemporary building accounts, contracts, household inventories and other relevant writings prohibits an exact reconstruction of room use in Blarney Castle, yet it is more likely that the 'Chapel', rather than fulfilling a liturgical role, served as the hall. As mentioned earlier in the chapter, there is evidence that a vault originally supported the floor level here. The internal arrangement of the hall being carried on the upper

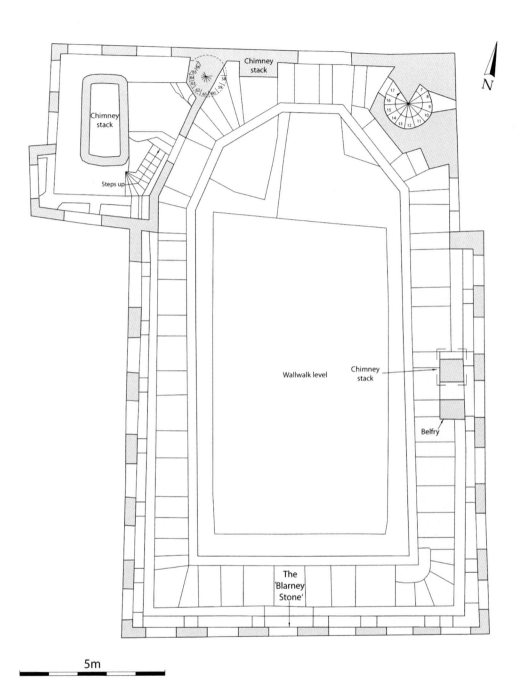

5m

3.39 The parapet level of Blarney Castle with its extensive machicolation along the east, south and west sides (surveyed by Hugh Kavanagh, courtesy of the Blarney Castle Estate).

3.40 The most distinctive feature of Blarney Castle is the battlements. No other tower house has such extensive machicolation, the stone superstructure that projects from the top of the castle. The machicolation protected castle defenders who would drop objects such as stones through holes between the supporting corbels onto attackers at the base of the wall. Such elaborate battlements also signalled the economic and social standing of the lords of Muskerry, an important consideration given their many Anglo-Irish and Gaelic rivals in the region. Note in the corner the distinctive form of the chimneystack, almost like a ship's funnel, which served the fireplaces in the 'Kitchen' (image courtesy of the Blarney Castle Estate).

vault, with the principal private chambers, the 'Family Room' and the 'Banqueting Hall' located between the lower and upper vaults, has been seen in other tower houses.[45] Typically, these halls on the upper floors of tower houses either possessed an open roof or a garret level, and indeed in the east and west walls of the 'Chapel' there are a number of flattened corbels that originally supported the timber trusses for the roof above. Very few roofs of medieval date survive in Ireland, though a comparable example may be found at a tower house in Dunsoghly, Co. Dublin. There is no inbuilt fireplace in the 'Chapel', suggesting that a centrally placed hearth heated the room, paralleling Luke Gernon's description of the Limerick hall where the fire was prepared in the middle of the chamber. Support for this interpretation is found with the lack of garret space over the MacCarthy hall, allowing the smoke to escape through an aperture in the original roof. This does not necessarily mean that the MacCarthys were oblivious to the merits of an inbuilt fireplace, as evidenced by the other examples to be found in the castle. One suspects that there was a cultural resonance to the display of a central hearth in the hall chamber compulsive enough to overcome the need for a fireplace.

3.41 Close-up view of the machicolation that projects externally from the top of the castle. This machicolation, supported on pyramidal corbels with slightly hollowed ogee-headed forms, creates an elegant profile for the castle.

The parapets

As mentioned above, another spiral stairwell opening off from the north end of the 'Chapel' allows access to the parapet level (figs 3.39 & 3.40). Unlike the stairwell that rose up through the body of the castle, the newel and steps in this instance are of rough construction. A flat-headed window in the east wall lights the progress of the stairwell, which terminates in a roof turret at parapet level. A flat-headed doorway, with a roughly dressed surround, allows access to an alure or walkway along the battlements of the tower house. The low parapet is crowned with machicolation, which is supported on pyramidal corbels with slightly hollowed ogee-headed profiles (fig. 3.41). The crenellation surmounting the machicolation possesses merlons that for the most part are stepped. Along the east wall, this machicolation stops short of the roof turret in the north-east corner and does not continue along the northern side of the parapet. The northern battlements on top of the sixteenth-century extension present a more irregular profile due to the presence of the roof turret and a chimneystack as well as the necessity to merge the parapet walls of the latter with those surmounting the earlier tower, which are lower. The alure inside the machicolation is rather narrow, consisting of flagstones set at an angle to allow for the

3.43 The round-arched bell-cote on the eastern battlements post-dates Gabriel Beranger's drawing of the castle in the 1770s. The north pilaster supporting the arch is built on top of a chimneystack that originally served the fireplaces in the 'Great Hall' and the 'Banqueting Hall'.

seepage of rainwater through drains provided at the foot of the low parapet walls. The side joints between these sloped flagstones are covered by capstones that make it more difficult to walk on the alure. The parapet walls with their drains (also known as weep holes) are hidden from spectators by the machicolation that projects by *c.*50cm. These parapet walls, with their low height, act as a foothold to allow for observation over the crenellated machicolation walls (fig. 3.42). There is a round-arched bell-cote midway along the top of the eastern battlements that post-dates Gabriel Beranger's drawing of the castle in the 1770s (fig. 1.10). The north pilaster supporting the arch is built on top of a chimneystack that served the fireplaces in the 'Great Hall' and the 'Banqueting Hall' (fig. 3.43). A second chimneystack located in the north-west corner of the battlements served the large fireplace in the 'Family Room'.

The parapets with their crenellation, roof turrets and machicolations were integral to the principles of castle architecture, both in a defensive and metaphorical sense. The appearance of such battlements created a sense of vulnerability for anyone approaching the immediate vicinity of the tower house. The metaphorical importance of the parapet can also be clearly illustrated in a Scottish laird's advice to his son not to build his house without battlements as the resulting edifice would be

3.42 (*opposite*) The wall-walk or alure inside the machicolation is rather narrow, with flagstones placed at an angle to allow for the seepage of rainwater through drains provided at the foot of the low parapet walls. The side joints between these sloped flagstones are covered by capstones that make it more difficult to walk upon. The parapet walls, with their low height, act as a foothold to allow for observation over the machicolation walls. The crenellation surmounting the machicolation possesses merlons that for the most part are stepped.

construed as demeaning to the family's heritage, undermining their standing in society.[46] To some extent, there are parallels with England, where the most striking aspect of most sixteenth- and early seventeenth-century buildings there are the elaborate rooflines. In Ireland and Scotland, however, there was an even sharper contrast between the rooflines and the lower elevations of the tower houses, which were more simple and mundane.[47]

Cormac 'Láidir' mac Taidhg's Castle: the late fifteenth-century tower

In the 1480s, a tall slender tower occupying the north-west corner of a bawn was first built at Blarney, after which it was decided to extend it, creating the towering monolith that can be seen today (figs 3.44–3.46). Judging by the similarities in the surrounds of the two-light ogee-headed windows on the upper floors of the two blocks, it is likely that this extension was built not long after in the early 1500s. This practice of building tower houses in two phases can be seen with a number of examples in Cos Limerick, Clare and Galway, though the integration of the earlier and later tower blocks at Blarney meant a greater provision of rooms than was typical for most tower houses. It is clear that while the hall chamber on the fourth floor facilitated the reception of guests and offered the principal room in which family members and their more esteemed guests could gather for meals, other chambers, including the smaller chambers in Cormac 'Láidir' mac Taidhg's tower, fulfilled less public roles. Such rooms could fulfil the functions of a great chamber, a withdrawing chamber or a bedroom and, as such, could be imbued with graded meanings of social exclusivity.

In general terms, certain rooms were accessible to a greater spectrum of the household than others. While estate workers could come and go in the service areas, access to the private apartments may have been restricted to the immediate family members, their guests and personal servants. Stops and pauses, and successive staging could allow for the communication of certain mentalities, certain meanings that underpinned relations both within a household and beyond. Thus the spatial arrangement of chambers could express in a real and meaningful way the social geography of a household. Socially conscious Victorians certainly recognized this and labelled the smaller chambers with names like the 'Young Ladies' Bedroom' or the 'Earl's Bedroom'. In this more private arena, the family would spend their leisure activity, including the entertainment of the more important guests. Pastimes would include singing, dancing, storytelling and feasting. Board games were favourites, as revealed in inventories, with games such as chess, backgammon, Fox and Geese and Nine Men's Morris being played.[48]

3.44 (*opposite*) This is the original tower that occupied the north-west corner of a bawn built in the 1480s by Cormac 'Láidir' mac Taidhg. In the early sixteenth century, his son Cormac Óg Láidir mac Cormaic extended Blarney Castle, creating the towering monolith that can be seen today. One of Blarney Castle's more attractive features is the oriel window that projects from the 'Earl's Bedroom'. Built of cut limestone, the oriel window dates to the early seventeenth century.

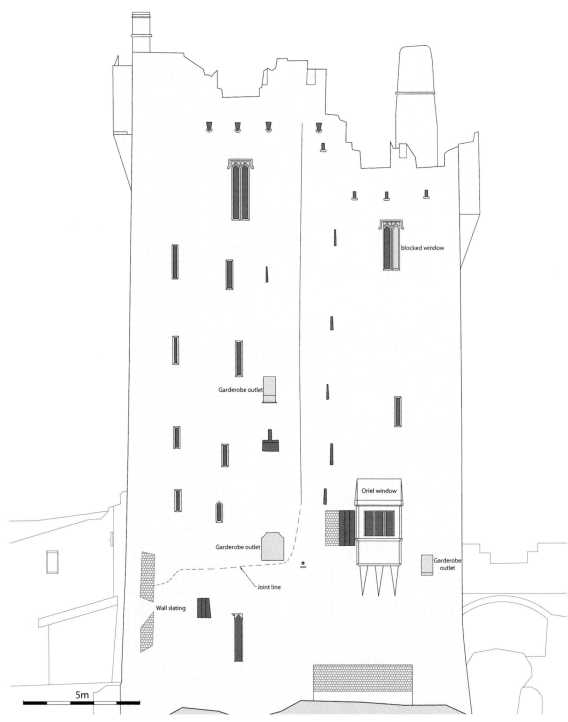

blocked window

Garderobe outlet

Oriel window

Garderobe outlet

Garderobe outlet

Joint line

Wall slating

5m

3.45 The north elevation of Blarney Castle. Judging by the similarities in the surrounds of the two-light ogee-headed windows on the upper floors of the two blocks, it is likely that the castle was extended in the early 1500s. Note the earlier castle wall still evident at ground-floor level underneath the extension (surveyed by Focus Surveys Ltd, prepared by Hugh Kavanagh, courtesy of the Blarney Castle Estate).

Original entry into Cormac 'Láidir' mac Taidhg's tower

As mentioned above, the original entrance for the late fifteenth-century tower no longer exists, though examination of the ground plan suggests that entry was gained in the east side of the building through a possible door embrasure located in the wall of a mural passage (fig. 3.16). This door embrasure was blocked with rubble masonry, which in turn was covered by plaster rendering. There is no evidence for any door surrounds, or other features such as a hanging eye or pivot-hole that would have held the original door. According to Crawford Woods, there were traces of an opening in the ceiling of this passage, but there is no evidence today to support this.[49] This mural passage/lobby area is provided with two flat-headed doorways, one allowing access into the ground-floor chamber of the earlier tower, the 'Earl's Bedroom'. The second doorway allows access into a small ante-chamber at the base of a spiral stairwell. A flat-headed window, lined with modern brick and protected with bars, was inserted into the north wall of this ante-chamber, providing lighting for the lobby area as a whole.

Moving into the 'Earl's Bedroom', the principle feature of this room is a large window inserted into an earlier timber-lintelled embrasure in the north wall (fig. 3.16). This five-light flat-headed window is contained within an oriel, built of limestone ashlar blocks, projecting from the exterior of the wall (fig. 3.44). This attractive addition is supported at its base by three pyramidal corbels and dates to the early seventeenth century, as evidenced by the window surrounds that are dressed with linear tooling typical of the period. There is a much-altered window embrasure in the west wall that serves a large aperture blocked with modern bars. Below the exterior of this opening is an earlier ope (now blocked), which is not evident from the interior due to remodelling of the embrasure to create a fireplace (fig. 3.29). A lintel slot and sloped back-wall have been inserted to facilitate this conversion. Smoke would have been guided through the existing aperture by the sloped back-wall and a now-disappeared fire-hood, which would have been supported by a lintel. In the south-west corner is an embrasure that facilitates two slit opes in the south wall. Another embrasure in the south wall serves a slit ope with a chamfered stone surround that is partially blocked. The sill of the embrasure possesses a reused piece of cut stone dressed with linear drafted margins. The room also has a pointed vault, covered with well-preserved rendering, with traces of wicker centring exposed in parts. In modern times, another flat-headed doorway with a timber lintel was mined through the fabric of the south wall at the south-east corner. This addition allows access between this room and the principal chamber on the first-floor level of the later tower, the 'Great Hall'.

The spiral stairwell that served the earlier tower is located in a slight projection at the north-east corner of the original building (fig. 3.47). Crawford Woods in 1896 noted that it was locally called the 'black stairs'.[50] This projection was swallowed up

with the extension of the castle, though one corner of it is still visible in the ancillary chambers that occupy the north end of the later tower block. The newel and steps are of rough construction, unlike the fine stairwell that was built in the sixteenth-century extension. From the base of the stairwell upwards, at every 360° turn, a flat-headed loop of rough construction in the north wall lights the progress of the stairs. This stairwell, in its upward progression, was also provided with three windows looking to the south-east. One of these windows, a flat-headed loop of rough construction, opens directly into an ancillary chamber at mezzanine level between the second and third floors of the later tower. The two other embrasures, between the ground and first floors, and the second and third floors of the first tower respectively, are now blocked. As such, the original appearance of these windows cannot now be ascertained.

Mezzanine level between ground and first floors of earlier tower

Only a short distance up the spiral stairwell that serves the early building, are a short flight of steps that have been subsequently mined through the thickness of the late fifteenth-century tower house (fig. 3.16). These steps descend a short distance to a flat-headed doorway, whose roughly dressed surround bears linear drafted margins. The remnants of iron hinges are present in the east jamb. This doorway allows access to a short corridor, which in turn connects with the spiral staircase of the sixteenth-century addition (see above, p. 61, for entry on connecting corridor between the two blocks).

Continuing up the spiral stairwell in the original tower, the visitor observes a flat-headed doorway opening off the stairs. After going through the doorway, one proceeds along a short corridor that terminates in a rather small room that acted as a garderobe chamber (fig. 3.20). A latrine chute can be seen in the floor at the north-west corner of the chamber. The latrine outlet is in the exterior of the north wall at ground-floor level. In the opposite, south-west, corner is a wall press. This chamber is lit by a single flat-headed loop with a roughly dressed surround in the west wall.

The 'Young Ladies' Bedroom': first floor of earlier tower

Further up the spiral stairwell is a double-centred doorway that allows access into the 'Young Ladies' Bedroom' (figs 3.22). The doorway itself is located in the north-east corner of the chamber that curves into the room to accommodate the stairwell. A second doorway, this time flat-headed, was mined into the south wall at the time that the castle was being extended in the sixteenth century. This subsequent opening allows access into a mural corridor built into the west wall of the later tower, which

3.46 (*opposite*) A view of the early tower from the south-west. Its enlargement into the castle that we see today suggests two things: an increase in the wealth of the lords of Muskerry; and an increasing need to express this power in a more manifest manner. The consolidation of MacCarthy control, particularly in the area around Blarney, against potential encroachment by the earls of Desmond and other Anglo-Irish families such as the Barretts and the Lombards in the early sixteenth century sets the background against which Blarney Castle was transformed.

in turn allows communication with the 'Family Room' (see above, pp 66–7, for entry on this corridor). The floor of the 'Young Ladies' Bedroom' has been largely removed, exposing the top of the vault that covers the ground-floor chamber below. The walls of this room are covered with two coats of well-preserved plaster rendering. In the west wall, there is the possible survival of an undercoat for a plaster frieze, similar in nature to the example seen in the 'Family Room', the principal second-floor chamber in the later tower. The room is lit by a number of openings, a flat-headed window in the north wall, an ogee-headed window in the west wall, a round-arched window in the south wall and a corner loop with ogee-shaped sill in the south-west corner (with only one original jamb remaining, the other replaced with later brickwork). The embrasure for the latter window has been mined through at its base to create a recess possibly for a fireplace (though unlike the example in the 'Earl's Bedroom', there is no provision for a lintel). The chamfered surrounds of these windows are roughly dressed. In the east wall, there is a blocked window embrasure that was presumably open before the extension of the castle. A number of corbels, principally in the north and south walls originally supported wall plates, which in turn carried a timber floor for the room above. Impressions of these wall plates can still be seen in the surviving internal rendering.

Castles have traditionally been seen as fundamentally masculine, reflecting the nature of the inheritance of land and power in late medieval and early modern Ireland through the male line, with marriage perceived as a means to consolidate and improve the social, financial and political standing of a family. While many women could be regarded as pawns in such arrangements, these alliances could still provide women of ability to become involved in affairs outside the confines of tower houses. The frequency of obituaries in the annals for the wives of even minor lords underlines the recognition given to the status of noble women within the native ruling classes.[51] In 1553, the daughter of O'Connor Faly, a native lord from east Offaly, travelled to England, 'relying on the number of her friends and relatives there and on her knowledge of the English language to request Queen Mary to restore her father to her, and on her appealing to her mercy, she obtained her father and brought him home'.[52] Agnes Campbell, the Scottish wife of Turlough Luineach, head of the O'Neills, played an integral role in the high politics of Ulster in this period. In one instance, she influenced her husband to accept the division of Tyrone between himself and the baron of Dungannon as proposed by the lord deputy of the time, Sir John Perrot, while she worked also to reach a final agreement between the Dublin government and the Scots in Antrim.[53] Such documented cases in the sixteenth century acknowledge the place of women in the maintenance of order and continuity within the Gaelic Irish political scene.[54]

Women in the early modern period were also actively involved, not only politically but economically as well. The wives of native lords could retain goods that they brought to their marriage, with some being entitled to receive income from the

3.47 The spiral stairwell that served the earlier tower was called the 'black stairs' by Victorians, presumably due to its more narrow proportions and poorer lighting compared to the stairwell in the later tower. A number of windows that originally lit the 'black stairs' were blocked up with the building of the extension, though one of these windows, a flat-headed loop, remains open, looking directly into an ancillary chamber of the later tower.

husband's lands for their own use. An example of this is the wife of MacCarthy Mór, who collected rent from his lands known as the *Cáin bheag*, or 'little tax'. Such women therefore had access to wealth and power independent of their male relatives.[55] Intriguingly, it would seem to be the case for the lesser native gentry that, by 1600, the wife provided the whole farming stock in the form of a dowry, with the husband only contributing the land.[56]

Tower houses as well as defensible strongholds were also family homes. It has been suggested that the smooth running of the household was the responsibility of the lady of the castle.[57] The stocking of food and other provisions came under the remit of the female head, as did dealing with many of the servants and workmen. This view of the domestic/private domain being the sole preserve of the 'household wife'

3.48 In the context of tower houses in Ireland, the 'Kitchen' in Blarney Castle is an unusual feature as, generally speaking, cooking appears to have taken place in a separate building, minimizing the threat of fire to the lordly residence. Two fireplaces were inserted into the uppermost floor of the early tower to facilitate cooking. The larger of the two occupies almost half of the original floor area of the chamber. To the left can be seen the smaller example, whose lintel projects from the wall, supported by rather plain corbels.

has been criticized as overly androcentric and stereotypical, ignoring the need for more sensitive discussion of intra-familial relations at this time.[58] However, with regard to the gendered ordering of space inside castles, the identification of precise room functions has remained problematic, since it is difficult to identify with certainty any rooms other than the hall and garderobes.[59] The hall is usually perceived as a masculine space, where the male head would have presided over the business of organizing political alliances and running country estates. The leading lady, however, may have ruled the activities of the household from this same chamber.

Many eulogies to these noble women testify to their generosity and hospitality, acting in a complimentary manner to the strength and determination of their husbands.[60] It is not without significance that in *c.*1620, when visiting a tower house, Luke Gernon was greeted by a lady with a retinue of attendants in the hall, where she performed a core role in providing hospitality. Ceremoniously, she would taste a variety of drinks before presenting each of them to Gernon, taking responsibility not only for their quality but also for the well-being of the guest.[61] Ladies of the castle were noted in the annals as providers of great hospitality. The Annals of the Four Masters in 1524 record Gormlaith, wife of Aodh O'Neill, as 'a most bounteous and hospitable woman who has bestowed many gifts upon … the literary men and ollaves', while in the same year, Mór, wife of Donnchadh O'Brien, is described as 'a woman who kept a house of open hospitality'.[62] Such accounts were not merely complimentary, as the hospitality exhibited by these women was fundamental in the creation and maintenance of legal, social, economic and political relations. Women as well as men were inextricably bound to displays of generosity and hospitality that credited the honour and status of a noble household.

Blarney Castle contained a household with men, women, boys and girls with attendant servants, again male and female. Despite the ascription of castle architecture as a metaphor for the masculine identity of the head of the household, the very activities of such gender-mixed households must have ascribed particular spaces and chambers with socially constructed notions of what counted for masculine and feminine, both in an explicit and implicit manner. Members of the household and visitors, on the basis of gender, could have a different understanding of what space was allowed to them and what was forbidden, and with this went different understandings of how to behave.

The 'Priest's Room': second floor of earlier tower

Still further up the stairwell, the second-floor chamber known as the 'Priest's Room' is accessed through a double-centred doorway (fig. 3.32). The doorway itself is located in the north-east corner of the chamber that also curves into the room to accommodate the stairwell. The walls of the 'Priest's Room' are covered with one to two coats of reasonably well-preserved rendering. Most of this is rather rough in texture, having clearly acted as an undercoat before a final, finer plaster finish was added to create a smooth wall face. The room is lit by a couple of openings, a round-arched window in the west wall and an ogee-headed window in the south wall. In the east wall there is a blocked window embrasure that was presumably open before the extension of the building in the sixteenth century. The room has a pointed barrel vault covered with rendering with traces of wicker centring again exposed.

The lack of documentary sources, such as contemporary building accounts and contracts, household inventories and other relevant writings, from either native or colonial sources, prohibits an exact reconstruction of room-use in such tower houses. Bearing in mind the evidence elucidated from other scholarly work on historic architecture in Ireland and Britain, however, chambers like the 'Priest's Room' can be interpreted as spaces to withdraw to from the hall, and as such were designed to cater for the daily needs of a wealthy household in the sixteenth and seventeenth centuries. Such rooms could fulfil the functions of a great chamber, a withdrawing chamber, a parlour, a bedroom or a privy chamber. These rooms, beyond the hall, have been termed 'private', though such spaces were not private in the sense of a domestic retreat in the modern manner. Important political functions could take place in these

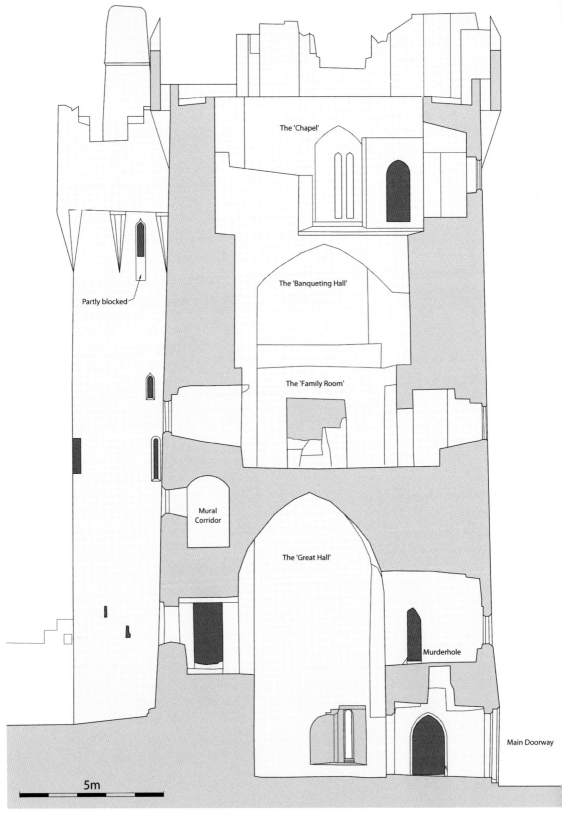

The 'Chapel'

Partly blocked

The 'Banqueting Hall'

The 'Family Room'

Mural
Corridor

The 'Great Hall'

Murderhole

Main Doorway

5m

3.49 Cross-section of castle, looking north. Compared to Georgian houses built in the eighteenth century, there is a general lack of symmetry in the apportioning of space and windows (surveyed by Focus Surveys Ltd and Hugh Kavanagh, courtesy of the Blarney Castle Estate).

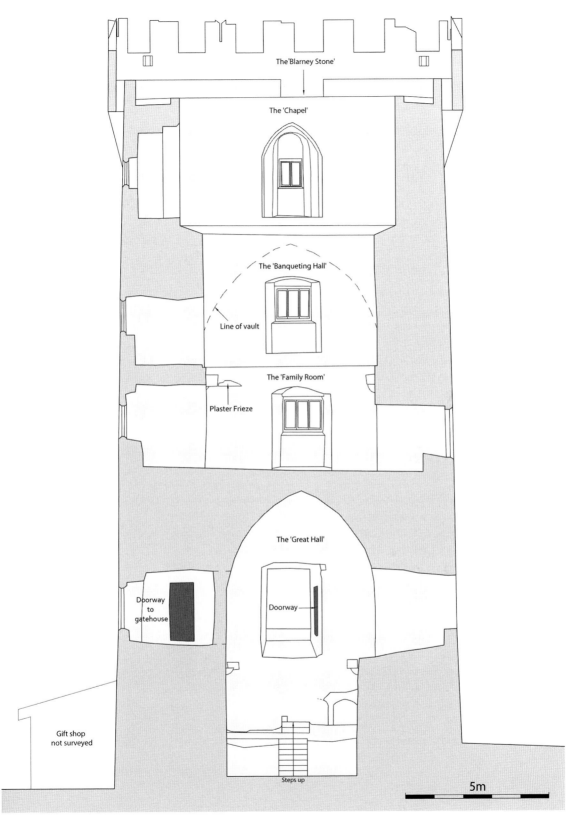

The 'Blarney Stone'

The 'Chapel'

The 'Banqueting Hall'

Line of vault

The 'Family Room'

Plaster Frieze

The 'Great Hall'

Doorway
to
gatehouse

Doorway

Gift shop
not surveyed

Steps up

5m

3.50 Cross-section of castle, looking south. Note that the walls of the tower house gradually become thinner the higher one goes, improving the stability of the building (surveyed by Focus Surveys Ltd and Hugh Kavanagh, courtesy of the Blarney Castle Estate).

rooms. Personal ties and connections were central to the flow of political power in the late medieval period. The family and household were a microcosm of political order and, as such, these rooms saw status and power played out at a more intimate level.

The 'Kitchen': third floor of earlier tower

The spiral stairwell eventually reaches the uppermost floor of the earlier tower via a double-centred doorway (fig. 3.37). The walls of the 'Kitchen' are largely bereft of rendering, revealing roughly coursed limestone rubble. The room is lit by a number of openings, a flat-headed window in the west wall and an ogee-headed window in the south wall. In the north wall, there is a rather fine twin-light, square-hooded, ogee-headed window with recessed spandrels. One of the lights has been blocked with fabric associated with the subsequent insertion of one of the two fireplaces in the room. These two lintelled fireplaces with substantial gatherings and flues were probably built at the same stage in the sixteenth century when the castle as a whole was being extended. The larger of the two fireplaces is massive, occupying almost half of the original floor area of the chamber (fig. 3.48). It consists of a three-part joggled flat arch, which is supported on either end by chamfered corbels that taper to pyramidal chamfer stops. Rising above a flat relief arch for this fireplace is a substantial chimneystack embellished with string-coursing. The second fireplace is a smaller affair, whose lintel projects from the south wall, supported by roughly dressed corbels of thin appearance. This fireplace abuts the south end of the larger fireplace, with its flue feeding into that of the larger example. In the process of inserting the larger fireplace, the window embrasures in both the north and south walls were partially infilled. In more recent times, the level of the room has been heightened with the insertion of a new cement floor. This new floor is provided with a drainage gully that allows for the seepage of rainwater out through the west window. The east wall of this chamber has been largely removed, with steps cut into the remaining fabric to allow access into the 'Chapel', via a double-centred doorway whose roughly dressed surround bears a chamfer rising from pyramidal stops. Examination of this doorway reveals its surrounds to be not only carved from a different source of limestone, but also dressed in a manner different from the other doorways in the castle. The wall fabric surrounding this door, which serves as a thin partition between the 'Kitchen' and the 'Chapel', is certainly not original either. This route of access between the third floor of the original tower and the fourth floor of the subsequent extension was contrived to facilitate the movement of visitors around the castle in modern times (fig. 3.37). A wall rebate supported by a chamfered limestone cornice originally held roof timbers over the chamber (certainly before the insertion of the fireplaces). A segmental arch with well-preserved traces of wicker centring springs over the south-east corner of the room. This arch supports the battlements of the later extension that partially run over the area of the original tower.

The parapets over Cormac 'Láidir' mac Taidhg's tower house

The spiral stairwell terminates in a roof turret at parapet level. A flat-headed doorway with a roughly dressed surround allows access to the alure along the battlements that crown the tower (fig. 3.39). A hanging eye and iron hinge are located inside the north jamb of this door. The parapet at the south-western corner is interrupted by machicolation that is supported by roughly dressed, chamfered pyramidal corbels. The parapet and the machicolation were built as a single unit. This machicolation stops just short of where the south wall of the original tower house meets the west wall of the subsequent addition. The alure inside the battlements is rather narrow, consisting of flagstones set at an angle to allow for the seepage of rainwater through drains provided at the foot of the parapet wall. The side joints between these sloped flagstones are covered by capstones that somewhat obstruct the alure in a manner similar to the walkway on the later tower block (fig. 3.42). The alure has not been interrupted by the subsequent insertion of the chimneystack, which took place sometime in the sixteenth century (figs 3.39 & 3.40). Unusually, this chimneystack is not open at the top, with the smoke instead allowed to escape only from a series of small openings just under the level of the string-coursing midway up the stack. Indeed at parapet level, the north and south sides of the chimneystack have been provided with a flat-headed window (now blocked) that opened out from the interior of the chimney flue, possibly to facilitate a greater draught (or possibly to facilitate the smoking of local produce from the surrounding estate, such as meat and cheese). There is a joint-line just above the level of the blocked windows, suggesting that the upper portion of the stack had been replaced or heightened at some stage, possibly in the early seventeenth century. At the south-east corner of the battlements, the alure rises in a series of steps to the battlements of the later tower block, the alure of which is at a considerably higher level.

CHAPTER 4

The 'transition' from castle to country house at Blarney

The seventeenth-century manor house

The early modern period in Ireland witnessed wide-ranging cultural, social, political and economic change, which transformed aspects of the material culture, including architecture. The native aristocracy who still held substantial estates sought to maintain their political and social standing in a society that was becoming increasingly anglicized with the arrival of more and more settlers from Britain, and not just in Ulster. The MacCarthys, lords of Muskerry, could not and did not remain oblivious to such changes. One obvious material manifestation of the new epoch was the rise of the country house, albeit in its earlier forms possessing defensive features that would not have looked out of place in tower houses. The Civil Survey of the 1650s records the presence of buildings in the vicinity of Blarney Castle including a 'new stone house, & stable, slated with a gatehouse'.[1] The MacCarthys probably built this 'new stone house' in the early decades of the seventeenth century in response to a desire for more extensive and convenient rooms than was possible by simply inserting larger, more fashionable windows into the tower house. Unfortunately, this building was removed by the construction of a new residence for the Jefferyes family during the eighteenth century (figs 1.3 & 1.10). Today, only two gun turrets to the east of the tower house testify to the past existence of this residence, integrated into the northern end of its eighteenth-century successor (figs 4.1 & 4.4). The fact that this house was provided with gun turrets suggests that this 'new stone house' was an example of a fortified manor house that evolved in the late sixteenth and early seventeenth centuries. Many manor houses were built by New English, Old English (as the Anglo-Irish came to be called at this time) and Gaelic Irish families in Co. Cork, including examples at Kanturk, Mallow and Monkstown (fig. 4.2). Scholars have considered the fortified examples as bridging the division between castle and house;[2] indeed, as a form of architectural compromise between the expectations of genteel living and the harsh political realities of the time.

The great variation in the plans and elevations of manor houses has challenged scholars, with little being done to explore more fully the social and cultural background of these buildings. Houses of L-, T- and U-plan are well known across the country. Houses with more basic oblong plans are embellished with tower projections, themselves either rectilinear, circular or spear-shaped. Doorways come

100

4.1 View of the north turret, one of two surviving turrets that are the only remains of a MacCarthy manor house integrated into the northern end of the later Georgian-Gothic mansion. The fact that the MacCarthy residence was provided with gun turrets suggests that it was an example of a fortified manor house that evolved in the late sixteenth and early seventeenth centuries in Ireland. This particular turret is equipped with gun loops on each of its two floors. Unusually, the chambers are covered by corbelled stone roofs and the gun loops possess a rather unique shape – a narrow slit with circular widening above the centre.

in a variety of shapes – flat-headed, double-centred, semi-circular or semi-elliptical – allowing access into the interior of these buildings. Windows take a variety of forms and sizes, though most are typically flat-headed, with the larger examples divided by mullions and transoms, and crowned by square hood-mouldings. In some buildings, the window surrounds appear to have been of timber rather than cut stone, precluding the identification of original forms. External string-coursing can highlight the different floors of these buildings, though in many cases this form of external decoration is limited to a single string-course defining the parapet level from the rest of the façade. The gable ends can be quite steep, sometimes rising into a chimneystack. In other instances, the chimneystacks themselves project from the gable ends or from the rear wall of the house. Chimneys can be grouped in rectangular stacks or set diagonally, sometimes panelled and with a cornice of oversailing stone-courses.

Despite the greater provision for well-lit domestic accommodation in manor houses, various defensive features found in them can be paralleled with those of tower houses. These include the small size of ground-floor or basement windows, the

4.2 View of Monkstown Castle, Co. Cork – a manor house built by the Archdeacon family in 1636, consisting of a central block flanked by square towers at each corner. It has recently been restored with the white-washed rendering applied to the exterior walls conveying an idea of how manor houses would have looked when they were first built. Such external rendering, being lime-based, is susceptible to the erosive effects of the weather.

provision of gun opes throughout the façades, and doors secured with large bolts, protected on the outside by a yett set into an external rebate and secured from within by a chain passing through an opening in one of the door jambs. Indeed, the vicinity of the entrance could be protected by the combination of a machicolation box at parapet level and gun opes inserted into the door jambs. A bawn wall embellished with a gatehouse, flanking gun turrets and numerous gun opes defended the approaches to many of these houses.

The architectural historian Maurice Craig has noted that the distribution pattern of seventeenth-century manor houses across Ireland is fairly random, though with empty patches, notably in southern Ulster. Many are to be found along the Shannon river basin, including north-east Galway, south Roscommon and the adjoining parts of Longford, Westmeath and Offaly. Tipperary has numerous such houses and there is a significant density in Co. Cork, along the Blackwater valley and the coastline. Furthermore, Craig is of the opinion that the total number of fortified manor houses including fragmentary remains is around 200, although the existing distribution is incomplete as far more houses have seen destruction over time, while many others lie hidden under the accretions of later building.[3] More recent analysis by Sharon Weadick suggests that 448 fortified manor houses, and nearly 500 possible examples, were actually built through the seventeenth century.[4] Even though there is a

4.3 The late medieval meets the early modern. At Leamanagh, Co. Clare, a fifteenth-century castle was extended with the building of a manor house against its side during the first half of the seventeenth century. The contrast between the tower house and manor house at this site in terms of form and space could hardly have been greater.

significant number of early modern buildings in Ireland, few are securely dated and they seem for the most part to be of post-1600 date.[5] Indeed, any manor house with secure dating invariably belongs to the first half of the seventeenth century, though their continued popularity into the post-Restoration era can be seen in the earl of Orrery's observation of 'the little old fashioned flankers such as most noble men and gentlemen's houses have to this day in Ireland'.[6]

The construction of a manor house with flanking gun turrets adjacent to Blarney Castle in the early decades of the seventeenth century has to be placed against a social, political and ideological background undergoing transformation. This period can be characterized as an anxious time for the native elite, including the MacCarthys of Muskerry, whose power base was under threat from officials in Dublin and London who sought to regularize their status according to the norms of common law and civil living. Moving into the localities were English Protestant landowners and settlers who, by example of their own lives, were to inspire natives to embrace civility and reformed religion. Such an agenda was to be supported by the introduction of English forms of tenure, estate organization, settlement and education. Social interaction between natives and newcomers through various means such as economic activity and the running of local government, however, allowed for the reciprocal exchange of ideas on social habits and customs. Such exchanges transformed both cultures, with both groups adjusting their cultural practices in the new environment.

The construction of a new house adjacent to Blarney Castle was not unique, as many tower houses were modified in the seventeenth and eighteenth centuries by the construction of an oblong extension, two to three storeys in height, built right up against one of the tower sides (fig. 4.3). These houses commonly equalled or surpassed in scale and prestige the earlier castles, with the latter being adapted and reshaped by succeeding generations, each alteration reflecting the architectural obsession of their day.[7] Yet, it is important to remember that the origins of building a house beside a castle are to be found in medieval times when halls often accompanied tower houses as part of an extensive complex. The Anglo-Irish castles at Askeaton and Newcastlewest, Co. Limerick, in the heart of the earldom of Desmond were provided in the fifteenth century with halls separate from the main residences. Barryscourt in east Co. Cork is a rather fine tower house of the sixteenth century, occupied by the Barrys, an Anglo-Irish magnate family in the region. Here, a stone and timber range abutted the north-west corner of the tower house with no means of direct communication between the two buildings. This separation of tower house and hall can be seen outside Munster as well. At Aughnanure, Co. Galway, a sixteenth-century stronghold of the O'Flahertys on the shores of Lough Corrib, there stand the remains of a masonry hall in the outer ward, with windows inserted into widely splayed embrasures spanned by stone arches bearing low-relief carvings of vine leaves and other ornamentation, similar to carvings found in the town houses of merchants in neighbouring Galway city.[8] At Blarney itself, the presence of a two-light ogee-headed window in the bawn wall associated with Cormac 'Láidir' mac Taidhg's earlier residence suggests the possibility that a substantial hall existed separate from the main tower house.

The testimony of sixteenth-century observers like Richard Stanihurst alludes to halls built adjacent to the tower houses of Gaelic Irish lords. According to Stanihurst,

> adjoining them [castles] are reasonably big and spacious palaces made of white clay and mud. They are not roofed with quarried slabs or slates, but with thatch. In the palace they have their banquets but they prefer to sleep in the castle rather than in the palace because their enemies can easily apply torches to the roofs.[9]

The Elizabethan antiquarian William Camden described Irish castles as

> no more than towers, with narrow loop-holes rather than windows; to which adjoins a hall made of turf, and roofed over with thatch, and a large yard fenced quite round with a ditch and hedge to defend their cattle from thieves.[10]

These accounts suggest that the halls were typically built of perishable material, such as posts-and-wattle and clay, and that they were roofed with thatch. As such, the archaeological evidence for such high-status buildings, even with excavation, can be

4.4 The north-west turret associated with the seventeenth-century manor house at Blarney also survives, though almost obscured by the walls of the later mansion.

quite ephemeral. Often the only evidence for the existence of such a hall is the scars of the roof left against the side of the tower house.

Traces of such a roof-scar can be seen in the east façade of the tower house at Blarney close to the north-east corner, though it could also be associated with the seventeenth-century manor house or its eighteenth-century Georgian-Gothic successor. The larger of the two turrets associated with the manor house is at the north end of the later mansion, built against the foot of the rock precipice, with the curved circumference on its external side facing northwards. Presently, the turret

4.5 The interior of the chamber within the north-west turret. It is D-shaped in plan and is covered with a stone corbelled roof. To the right is an embrasure for a gun loop facing west and to the left is the entrance to a short cave that continues underneath the castle. The surface of the wall is now covered with a calcium carbonate dissolved from the limestone wall fabric.

contains two storeys, but a third floor may have been removed with the construction of the eighteenth-century mansion.[11] The surviving uppermost level of this turret is splayed outwards to take the original north gable-end of the seventeenth-century manor house. In modern times, a round-arched entranceway has been mined through the north side of the turret allowing access into the ground-floor area (fig. 4.1). This has skewed the original internal arrangements inside this structure, which are as follows: a stairwell in the east side rises steeply into the body of the neo-Gothic Georgian mansion but was blocked up with masonry and mortar at some stage in the nineteenth century.[12] At the base of this stairwell is a small ante-chamber through which a ground-floor chamber is accessed via a flat-headed doorway of rather basic appearance but with a rather high sill. The ground-floor chamber of the turret is irregular in plan with a corbelled roof, and the floor is obscured by a considerable amount of stone rubble. On both the north-east and the south-east sides of this chamber is a lintelled double splayed gun loop, with the outer splay of the embrasure blocked up. Another stairwell in the west side of the turret, placed parallel to the aforementioned example, is a later addition, inserted at the same time as the round-arched entranceway. The insertion of this later stairwell has removed the floor of a passage that originally allowed access to the first-floor chamber, a room also irregular in plan with a corbelled roof. This chamber is provided with three similar lintelled

4.6 Immediately east of the tower house is a rock precipice against which the Georgian-Gothic mansion was built at a lower level. This mansion, which was originally four storeys in height, was built in the mid-eighteenth century by the new owners of Blarney Castle, the Jefferyes family, on the site of the earlier fortified manor house. All that remains of this mansion is a tall campanile-style round tower that dominates the ruined front façade.

double-splayed gun loops in the north wall. The appearance of these gun loops is unique, as they consist of a very narrow vertical slit with a circular widening above centre. The first-floor passage continues in the opposite direction for a considerable length to the south-west, giving entry into the ground-floor chamber of the second turret. Intriguingly, this passage is roofed with lintels, some of which are sills from mullioned windows, possibly derived from renovations carried out in the tower house in the late sixteenth/early seventeenth century. The second turret is also incorporated into the walls of the later mansion (fig. 4.4). The ground-floor chamber in this turret is D-shaped in plan, with a corbelled roof and a lintelled double-splayed gun loop facing west. The aforementioned passage continues beyond the ground-floor chamber to the south-west, where it allows access to a long narrow cave that terminates in a naturally formed chamber underneath the tower house (fig. 4.5).

Given the evidence from Blarney Castle and elsewhere, it is clear that there was a transformation in the nature of elite identity by the early seventeenth century, with such changes being mediated and expressed in novel forms of spatial organization that embodied polite disposition. The physical appearance of the seventeenth-century manor house at Blarney is not known, though the presence of two turrets to the north and north-west suggest a building whose layout and plan may have been unique to the area. This fortified manor house, probably built during the tenure of

Cormac Óg, Viscount Muskerry (1616–40), however, did not remain as the core residence of Muskerry MacCarthys. As mentioned in chapter one, it appears that Macroom Castle, further west in the Lee valley, served as the main residence for the family from the mid-seventeenth century onwards, for it was here that Giovanni Battista Rinuccini, the papal legate, was entertained for a week in 1645 and it was here that the MacCarthys, as earls of Clancarty, were to return after the Restoration.[13] Blarney Castle may have continued to be used as a secondary residence that could be leased periodically. During the 1680s, the Revd Roland Davies, Anglican rector of the local parish, resided in Blarney Castle as a tenant of Lady MacCarthy.[14]

The Georgian-Gothic mansion and the surrounding demesne gardens

Immediately east of the terrace between the gatehouse and the tower house is a rock precipice against which the Georgian-Gothic mansion was built at a lower level. This mansion was built in the mid-eighteenth century by the Jefferyes family on the site of the earlier fortified manor house (fig. 4.6).[15] The north end of the later mansion overlies the two gun turrets associated with the seventeenth-century residence (figs 4.1 & 4.4). Little now remains of this Georgian-Gothic mansion except for a much altered shell that survives only to two storeys in height. Various antiquarian views depict the building as a four-storey edifice with three to four towers projecting from its eastern and northern façades. This house, finely depicted by Gabriel Beranger in a drawing of c.1775–7, is considered to be one of the earliest appearances of neo-Gothic architecture in Ireland, which in this instance saw a fusion of Gothic and Georgian classical design (fig. 1.10). It is rather haphazard in plan, which possibly betrays the imprint of the earlier manor-house. The Jefferyes family laid out a landscape garden known as the 'Rock Close' and this, together with the demesne parkland decorated with statues and a picturesque pseudo-dolmen, attracted the attention of painters and poets. Within the grounds of the estate are a number of structures typically associated with an eighteenth-century demesne including three lime kilns and two ice-houses as well as garden follies. Besides the tall campanile-style round tower placed against the east façade of the much ruined Georgian-Gothic house (fig. 4.6), two other towers were constructed by the Jefferyes family in the surrounding gardens, namely the 'Lookout Tower' and the 'Keeper's Watchtower'.[16]

Follies and other garden buildings vary greatly in design and form, with Palladianism, Gothic Revival and prehistoric primitivism, among a number of influences, providing inspiration.[17] These garden features can vary in design and appearance, and include grottoes, obelisks, columns, sham castles, gazebos, towers and temples, as well as (in some instances) gates, lodges and bridges.[18] The *Oxford English dictionary* defines a folly as 'a building erected for no definite purpose; a costly structure apparently built for fantastic reasons, or a useless and generally

4.7 View of the 'Lookout Tower'. The interior of this turret, covered with a stone corbelled roof, is bereft of any other features such as windows or gun opes. There are no indications to suggest that this turret formed the south-west corner of a rather large bawn. Instead, it is more likely that this turret is a post-1700 garden folly erected during a programme of demesne landscaping. Follies were created to facilitate the enjoyment of parklands, gardens and other scenic views.

foolish building erected in the grounds of a wealthy eccentric'.[19] It has been suggested that while the above description has some level of truth, many of the most outrageous follies may have created a setting appropriate for sitting down to enjoy a view or consume tea. Indeed, such buildings may also have provided venues for banquets, writing or contemplation, as well as evoke memories of past events or deceased loved ones.[20]

The 'Lookout Tower' stands isolated *c.*8om to the south-west of Blarney Castle on top of a rock outcrop (fig. 4.7). It is one storey in height, built of roughly coursed limestone rubble. It is accessed through a simple pointed doorway with no dressed surround. A number of stones project from the wall surrounding the doorway. The interior of this turret, roofed with a corbelled vault, is bereft of any other features including windows or gun opes. There are no indications in the wall fabric to suggest

4.8 In the foreground is the campanile-style round tower associated with the Georgian-Gothic mansion, while in the background is the 'Keeper's Watchtower'. The provision of such towers suggests that the Jefferyes family favoured the development of various vantage points to appreciate the surrounding demesne with its attractive setting of the castle, parkland and rivers. The windows of the 'Keeper's Watchtower' do not overlook the river as one would expect for a defensive tower, but instead its large windows allowed observers to take in the view of the eighteenth-century mansion framed by the impressive silhouette of Blarney Castle.

that this turret formed the south-west corner of a rather large bawn. Instead, the structure's layout and fabric suggests that this turret is a post-1700 garden folly erected in a programme of demesne landscaping.

The circular tower, the 'Keeper's Watchtower' stands in isolation *c.*40m north-east of the tower house, built into the rise of an east-facing slope (fig. 4.8). It is three storeys in height, built of regularly coursed limestone rubble that has been largely re-pointed in recent times. The ground floor of an earlier structure remains, which is roughly circular in plan with a flattened north-east side, the broken east end of which continues beyond the circumference of the tower above and forms the north jamb of a segmental-headed doorway in the east side of same tower. Another entrance in the west side of the tower, a flat-headed doorway with timber lintel, allows access into the ground floor. This doorway appears to be heavily repaired, with the surrounding wall

4.9 The Georgian-Gothic mansion was burnt in a fire in 1820, forcing the Jefferyes family to leave Blarney and to relocate to Inishera House in east Cork. The Blarney estate passed by marriage in 1846 to the Colthurst family, who returned to Blarney in 1874, building a Scottish baronial mansion in the vicinity of Blarney Castle. This fine residence was designed by the architect John Lanyon and remains the home of the Colthurst family.

fabric containing brick inclusions. After going through this doorway, one encounters a landing with a short flight of stone steps leading down to the ground level within. This ground-floor level is provided with two windows in the east side, a slit ope (now blocked) and a flat-headed window with chamfered stone surround, dressed with linear tooling. From the aforementioned landing, a now disappeared wooden newel stairwell originally allowed access to the first-floor level of the tower, as indicated by joist holes in the internal wall fabric. Both the first- and second-floor levels were provided with large flat-headed windows in the west wall, each crowned with timber lintels.

The Jefferyes family, in the manner of improving landlords, also set about transforming the nearby village of Blarney into a small manufacturing centre. In 1765, a linen mill, twenty-five weavers' cottages and a bleaching green were constructed, creating the basis for further expansion in later years. The present appearance of Blarney village, with houses arranged around a square, dates from this period. A fire enveloped the Georgian-Gothic mansion in 1820, forcing the Jefferyeses to leave Blarney and relocate to Inishera House in east Cork. The latter house has since been demolished. The Blarney estate passed by marriage to the Colthurst family in 1846, who returned to Blarney in 1874, building a Scottish baronial mansion *c.*200m south of Blarney Castle (fig. 4.9). This fine residence was designed by John Lanyon and remains the home of the Colthurst family.[21]

CHAPTER 5

The chronology of Blarney Castle's development

Introduction

The dating of individual tower houses can be difficult to establish with any degree of precision, as exemplified by A.J. Jordan's work on the chronology of tower houses in Co. Wexford.[1] But, what we do know is that after a tall slender tower was first built at Blarney in the 1480s it was decided to extend it, creating the towering monolith that can be seen today (fig. 5.1). Judging by the similarities in the surrounds of the two-light ogee-headed windows on the upper floors of the two blocks, it is likely that this extension was built not long after. This practice of building tower houses in two phases can be seen with a number of examples in Cos Limerick, Clare and Galway. First, the block with entrance, spiral stairwell and ancillary chambers was constructed. This was followed by the addition of the larger block containing the principal rooms such as the hall chamber. From a structural perspective, it could be argued that a tower house built in two sections may absorb stress more efficiently, limiting potential subsidence of the walls. Yet, the horizontal stone courses and inner rubble fill of tower houses in general can absorb stress more readily than modern buildings constructed of concrete.[2] It is more likely the case that such sectional buildings were constructed over a number of seasons, depending on the resources available. This two-phase, two-part construction strategy that can be seen in a number of tower houses in the west of Ireland, however, should not be confused with the situation at Blarney, where a small, self-contained tower house was extended as an afterthought.[3] The fact that the east façade of the original tower was provided with openings that were subsequently built over proves this to be the case.

In the instance of Blarney Castle, the first tower was a fully functional tower house occupying the north-west corner of a bawn. It was then decided to build an extension containing much larger chambers, ancillary chambers and garderobe chambers, all linked by a separate stairwell. The addition of substantial living space suitable for the needs of a lordly household suggests two things: an increase in the economic power of the Muskerry MacCarthys, and an increasing need to articulate this power in a more manifest, permanent manner. The consolidation of the borders of Muskerry, particularly in the area around Blarney, against potential encroachment by the earls of Desmond, and other long-established Anglo-Irish families such as the Barretts and the Lombards, after the Battle of Mourne Abbey in 1521, may actually

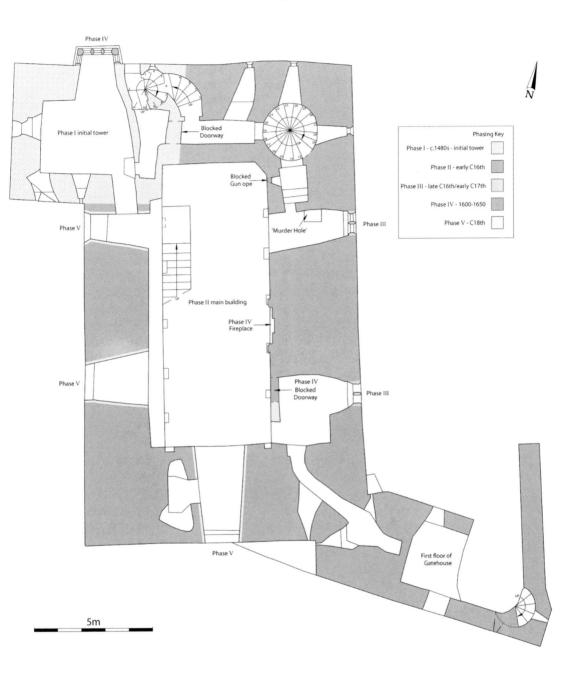

Phase IV

Phase I initial tower

Blocked Doorway

Blocked Gun ope

Phase V

'Murder Hole'

Phase III

Phase II main building

Phase IV Fireplace

Phase V

Phase IV Blocked Doorway

Phase III

Phase V

First floor of Gatehouse

N

Phasing Key

Phase I - c.1480s - initial tower

Phase II - early C16th

Phase III - late C16th/early C17th

Phase IV - 1600-1650

Phase V - C18th

5m

5.1 This first-floor plan of Blarney Castle illustrates the chronological development of the tower house, with its initial extent in the 1480s, followed by a major expansion in the early sixteenth century. In the late sixteenth or early seventeenth century, square-hooded windows were inserted. At some stage in the first half of the seventeenth century, a classical fireplace was put into the 'Great Hall', and an oriel window into the north wall of the 'Earl's Bedroom'. Finally, in the eighteenth century, large windows were inserted into the south and west walls.

provide the background against which Blarney Castle was transformed. A fortified MacCarthy border post constructed by Cormac 'Láidir' mac Taidhg on the fringes of Muskerry, now under his son Cormac Óg Láidir mac Cormaic, became the family residence at the heart of this Gaelic lordship.

Previous discussion on Blarney

Despite Blarney Castle's prominence in popular literature on Irish castles, relatively little informed discussion has been published on the architecture and chronological development of the building. A number of commentators have proffered opinions on the chronology of Blarney Castle. Cecil Crawford Woods noted that the wall of the original bawn that accompanied the earlier tower was incorporated into the north façade of the extension overlooking the precipice.[4] Mike Salter, Mark Samuel and Kate Hamlyn regard the machicolation gracing the battlements as a later addition with the stub of the original parapet now forming a step in the alure.[5] Indeed, the machicolation (or bartizan as Salter terms it) above the earlier tower is seen as being associated with the remodelling of the castle in the 1590s, which also saw the insertion of two- and three-light square-hooded mullioned windows into the three upper floors of the later tower house.[6] However, inspection of the parapets suggests that the machicolated battlements on both towers are original features and are not the result of subsequent renovations. Indeed, Salter's date of the 1590s for the insertion of the square-hooded windows is rather too refined, given that these windows could have been inserted at any time from the late sixteenth to the mid-seventeenth century. James Healy regards the later tower as being constructed towards the end of the fifteenth century, while the battlements are later again, possibly of late sixteenth- or early seventeenth-century provenance.[7] John Collins regards the larger tower block as being erected during the tenure of Sir Cormac Mac Taidhg (1571–83), incorporating the earlier tower, which had been built about a century previously.[8] The same author sees many structural alterations (presumably the insertion of the classical fireplace and square-hooded windows) as likely to have taken place during the time of Cormac Óg of Kilcrea, the first Viscount Muskerry (1616–40).[9]

It is of particular interest that many window and door surrounds in tower houses are treated with a dressing of punching, often in a delicate manner. It is assumed that this punching allowed for rendering to adhere onto what otherwise would be a smooth surface, making it easier for the finish to stay in place. Cognisance of dated buildings bearing such decorated stonework has allowed for the outline of a developmental sequence in the type of punching used from the late fifteenth to the early seventeenth century. The earlier work is characterized by a dressing of fine punch-marks, sometimes arranged in fine lines. By the mid-sixteenth century, the punch-work was been used as a design on the stone surrounds of doorways and

5.2 Example of late medieval stone dressing on the lower left-hand side of the entrance to Blarney Castle. Many window and door surrounds in tower houses are treated with a dressing of punching, often in a delicate manner. It is assumed that this punching allowed for plasterwork to adhere to what otherwise would be a smooth surface, making it easier for the finish to stay in place. In some instances, this punching was arranged in a decorative manner in the form of geometric patterns, suggesting that such window and door surrounds may have been left uncovered.

windows, with heavy punching, usually set in bands, framed by outer rows of finer bands. By the late sixteenth century, masons were using punching to create decorative geometric motifs.[10]

The trouble with the above sequence is that in many tower houses, the door and window surrounds do not bear such attractive punching. Instead, they are roughly dressed, making it difficult to ascertain an accurate relative date. Blarney Castle is no exception in this regard; the limestone surrounds of the pointed doorways in both the earlier and later tower blocks are roughly dressed with no discernible pattern of punching that could be used to date the development of the building. Indeed, the similarities in the dressing of stonework in both parts of the building suggest that there was no substantial time-lag between the construction of the original tower in the late fifteenth century and its subsequent expansion. The only exceptions are the arched doorways serving the lobby area and the example in the west wall of the 'Family Room', where portions of the jambs and lintel are dressed with fine punch-marks arranged in fine lines, typical of the fifteenth and early sixteenth centuries, as discussed above (fig. 5.2).

The chronological development of Blarney Castle

It has been pointed out that the timber sill still preserved in one of the window embrasures of the 'Young Ladies' Bedroom' may allow the early tower to be accurately dated by scientific methods such as dendro- or radiocarbon-dating.[11] Radiocarbon-dating is notoriously imprecise for the early modern period. Dendro-dating (dendrochronology: the counting of tree rings in samples of oak) is also limited, given the rare survival of woodwork such as flooring or roofing used in the primary construction of buildings. Given the difficulties in closely dating the original construction of specific tower houses and any alterations made thereafter, on the basis of the present survey, the following chronology is proposed for Blarney Castle (fig. 5.1):

Phase I: c.1480s

It was under the chieftainship of Cormac 'Láidir' mac Taidhg (1461–95) that the tall slender four-storey tower was constructed on the rock outcrop overlooking the meeting of the Martin and Blarney rivers. This tower formed the north-west corner of a bawn, of which little survives except for portion of its northern length preserved in the later extension, and the footings of its southern and western circuit that run under the same extension (figs 3.13 & 5.3). It has been suggested that the footings projecting from the south façade of the tower house may in fact belong to a tower that would have occupied the south-west corner of the original bawn, an intriguing possibility that remains to be proven.[12] The relatively early date of this tower is indicated by the rather small and crude windows that served the interior, except for the uppermost floor. Tower houses built in this period tended to be provided with rather small opes, except for the uppermost level, where the hall chamber would be. At this level, a two-light ogee-headed window is located in the north wall of the Blarney tower and its square hood-moulding, the pronounced spandrels and the rough surface dressing tie in with a late fifteenth-century date.

Phase II: early sixteenth century

Within a generation or so, it was decided that the amount of living space inside the tower was not suitable for the large extended household of the Muskerry MacCarthys.

5.3 When first constructed by Cormac 'Láidir' mac Taidhg (1461–95), Blarney Castle was a much smaller affair, consisting of a tall slender four-storey tower, situated at the north-west corner of a walled courtyard or bawn. This bawn was largely demolished following the castle's enlargement in the early sixteenth century, though its footings are visible along the south (seen here) and west sides of the tower house. A portion of it is also preserved in the north façade of the castle (see fig. 3.13).

It is possible that during the tenure of Cormac Óg Láidir mac Cormaic (1501–36) the later extension was constructed over the area of the bawn, enveloping the eastern and southern walls of the earlier tower. The south-east corner of the original tower can be seen projecting into the main chambers inside the later extension (fig. 3.33). In addition, the corner of the projecting stairwell that served the earlier tower can be seen in the ancillary chambers of the later tower house (fig. 3.31). Access into the tower house was regulated through a multi-storey gatehouse abutting the south-east corner of the building. Also at some stage in the sixteenth century, two fireplaces were inserted into the old hall chamber of the earlier tower, converting this most eminent chamber into a mere 'kitchen'. Given the size of one of the fireplaces, which in effect now occupied half of the room, a substantial chimneystack was put in place, crowning the tower and displaying to all and sundry in the locality the lordly munificence of a household that required such extensive cooking facilities. It is important to remember, however, that the passage that now exists between the 'Kitchen' and the 'Chapel' did not exist until relatively recent times. The nearest principal chamber to the 'Kitchen' would have been the 'Family Room', two floors down.

The chimneystack on top of the early tower was remodelled and bequeathed with a slanted profile in the manner of a ship's funnel (fig. 3.40). This was marked off with string-coursing, which is typical of *c*.1600. A new bawn was constructed to the west of the castle with its rather wide wall-walk and crenellated battlements with each merlon provided with a gun ope typical of the period (fig. 3.4). A two-storey gun turret at the north-west corner of the bawn was accessed from the wall-walk via a flat-headed doorway with a chamfered stone surround dressed with linear tooling, such dressing again pointing to a late sixteenth-/seventeenth-century date (fig. 3.6). This turret was integrated into the rest of the bawn wall, leaving no doubt that this courtyard was laid out *c*.1600. Indeed, this could be the very bawn referred to as 'four piles joined into one' in the *Pacata Hibernia*. Given that this was a period in which genteel living was espoused, it should come as no surprise that the medieval spaces inside the castle were remodelled. The ogee-headed windows in the main chambers were replaced with square-hooded, mullioned windows, providing more light for those within and tantalizing glimpses of luxuries for those outside. Furthermore, the vault over the 'Banqueting Hall' was replaced with a timber floor, creating a more spacious, airy room. The placing of the three-light windows solely on the second and third floors suggests an increased emphasis on the lower floors. This is a reflection of a larger cultural trend that saw the relegation of the hall chamber and its replacement by the great chamber as the principal space for a landed household. Now, the great chamber and other pre-eminent spaces were located on the lower floor levels, and it is apparent that such a process was being replicated at Blarney. The fact that the finest fireplace in the castle is to be found at first-floor level is not without coincidence.

The first floor of the castle is finally acknowledged as one of the pre-eminent spaces in the early decades of the seventeenth century. A classical fireplace, one of the finest earliest classical representations to be found in Co. Cork, was inserted into the vaulted first-floor room (fig. 3.19). This floor now served either as a great chamber or maybe as a more exclusive parlour chamber. The form of the mantelpiece, with its classical entablature, compares closely to a similar example found in a manor house at Monkstown, Co. Cork, bearing the date 1636. Oriel windows are rare in Irish tower houses, and the Blarney example (fig. 3.44) has been compared to one found at Granagh Castle, a Butler residence in Co. Kilkenny. Indeed, it has been suggested that the oriel window dates to the chieftainship of Tadhg mac Cormaic Óig MacCarthy (1536–65), whose daughter Julia married, as her third husband, Edmund Butler, Lord Dunboyne, brother of the earl of Ormond, holder of Granagh Castle.[13] The family link with Granagh may have influenced Tadhg mac Cormaic Óig to adopt a similar architectural device for his residence. Yet comparison of the two oriel windows demonstrates significant differences. The Granagh example bears segmental-headed windows placed within a box built of rubble construction, while the example that lights the 'Earl's Bedroom' has flat-headed windows, and is contained within an ashlar-built projection. This oriel in turn is supported at its base by three pyramidal corbels, while the base of the Granagh example tapers to a point. This attractive addition at Blarney dates to the first half of the seventeenth century, as evidenced by the window surrounds that are covered with linear tooling characteristic of the time. Indeed, Harold Leask ascribes a seventeenth-century date to the example of Granagh too.[14] Without doubt, the insertion of this oriel window and the classical fireplace took place in the context of the 'new stone house' constructed beside the castle before the Cromwellian reconquest of the 1650s. Little now survives of this manor house except for the remnants of two turrets to the north and north-west. The gatehouse was also renovated at this time, with the insertion of a round-arched doorway. It is likely that the seventeenth-century residence occupied the footprint of the Georgian-Gothic mansion that replaced it by the middle of the eighteenth century. It is clear that by the 1650s Blarney Castle had ceased to be the main residence of the MacCarthy family, who subsequently, as earls of Clancarty, preferred to dwell at their other castle at Macroom. Unfortunately, nothing survives of their residence at Macroom, because this could have provided some insight into the original appearance of the 'new stone house' recorded at Blarney in the 1650s.

Phase V: eighteenth century

The mid-eighteenth century saw the erection of a four-storey residence on the location of the older manor house. This new building, designed in a Georgian-Gothic style, represented one of the earliest expressions of neo-Gothic architecture in Ireland. Various antiquarian views depict a four-storey residence embellished with a number of towers, two of which retained the lower floors of the turrets associated with the earlier manor house on the site. Little survives of this fine Georgian-Gothic building, the original fire and its aftermath saw much of its interior gutted, while over the decades the surviving façades have gradually become obscured by ivy growth. Attempts to improve the stability and appearance of this building a number of decades ago obscured the original Georgian-Gothic façade, though some of the original window openings (now blocked) remain. The tower house itself saw some improvements in the eighteenth century: the first floor saw the insertion of large window embrasures; while the opening of the classical fireplace was filled in with brick to create a much smaller fireplace. The floor above, the 'Family Room', saw its great fireplace reduced to more suitable dimensions. The lower walls of the tower house were also graced with exterior slate-hanging. These improvements may be due to the efforts of one Mr Beer, who resided as a tenant in the tower house in 1750, or alternatively to the activities of George Charles Jefferyes and his wife Anne La Touche in 1797.[15]

Introduction

Blarney Castle is one of the largest examples of a type of castle called the tower house. Such castles, built between the fifteenth and seventeenth centuries, are a common sight in the Irish countryside. They are typically rectilinear in plan, and range from four to five storeys in height, with the roofline crowned with battlements. The very essence of such tower houses is the vertical arrangement of living space within. A ground floor entrance, usually in the form of an arched doorway with a punch-dressed surround, allows access into a lobby area. This lobby is covered by a murder hole (as at Blarney), and from this area one can access a spiral stairwell to the floors above. Alternatively, one can turn into a small guardroom chamber flanking the entrance, or proceed straight ahead into a ground floor chamber. The spiral stairwell ascends from one corner of the tower house in a clockwise fashion to parapet level, with each of the floors accessed via a doorway off the stairs. It is not unusual, though, for the stairwell to terminate at the uppermost room and for another stairs in that room to give access to the roof instead (like at Blarney). The upper floors are usually provided with larger, more ornate windows, fireplaces and garderobes (toilet chambers). Vaulting can support one or two floors, but in later tower houses wooden flooring is used throughout the building. Windows come in a variety of shapes and sizes, but are typically flat-, round- or ogee-headed, with the larger examples divided into a number of lights with mullions (vertical bars) and transoms (horizontal bars). Both the internal and external wall surfaces of tower houses were originally covered with plaster that protected the walls from the elements. The plaster was often white.

The bawn

Unlike the large castle that can be seen today, the original tower house built in the 1480s by Cormac 'Laidir' mac Taidhg, the sixth MacCarthy lord of Muskerry (1461–95), consisted of a tall slender tower, four storeys in height, dominating one corner of a walled courtyard (known as a bawn). Traces of this bawn are still visible in the north, west and south walls of the present building. The original tower survives as the block projecting from the northwest corner of the castle. At some stage in the early sixteenth century, probably during the tenure of the Cormac Óg Láidir mac Cormaic, the ninth lord of Muskerry (1501–36), the east and south sides of this tower were greatly extended by the building of a five-storey tower block on the site of the accompanying bawn. This necessitated the laying out of a new bawn to the west of Blarney Castle, of which the north wall and a corner turret survive.

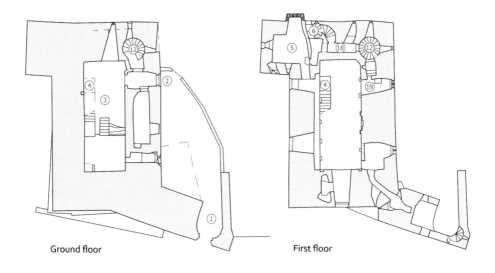

Ground floor

First floor

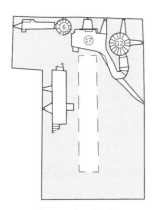

Intermediate level

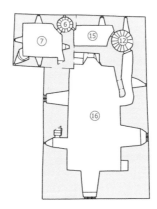

Second floor

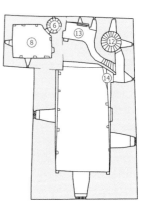

Third floor

Walking guide to Blarney Castle

1 Gate house
2 Main doorway
3 Ground floor chamber
4 The 'Great Hall'
5 The 'Earl's Bedroom'
6 The 'black stairs'
7 The 'Young Ladies' Bedroom'
8 The 'Priest's Room'
9 The 'Kitchen'
10 Battlements and the 'Blarney Stone'
11 The 'Chapel'
12 spiral stairs
13 Garderobe
14 The 'Banqueting Hall'
15 Ancillary chamber
16 The 'Family Room'
17 Garderobe
18 Corridor
19 Murder-hole

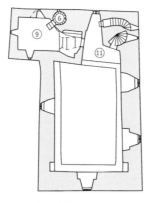

Fourth floor

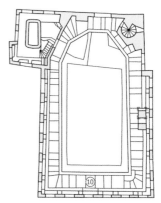

Wallwalk level

① The gatehouse

On approaching Blarney Castle, one encounters a two-storey gatehouse of early sixteenth-century date. The entrance is rather ornate – a round-arched doorway with an attractive stone-cut surround – but it is probably seventeenth century in date, judging from its appearance. The arch is contained within a square hood moulding. The doorway possesses an external grille, known to architectural experts as a yett, which could be closed over the doorway in case of attack. Photographs taken of the castle in the Victorian era indicate that the doorway was missing before being put back in place sometime in the late nineteenth century. On passing through the doorway, one can see into the first floor above. This room possesses a barrel vault which suggests that the gatehouse was at least another storey higher originally. In the corner of this room, one can see the base of a spiral stairs that would have allowed access to this higher floor level.

② Entrance into the tower house

Going through the gatehouse, one is admitted onto a narrow terrace that flanks the eastern side of the tower house. At the far end of the terrace is an arched doorway that allows entry into the interior of the tower house. This doorway has a recess in its stone surround that also allowed it to carry a yett that could be pulled over the doorway in times of danger. The hinges for this can still be seen in the right-hand jamb of the entrance. On passing through this arched doorway, one enters a lobby with three arched doorways opening off it. The doorway to the left gives entry to a small guardroom chamber with an arched vault and blocked window; while the doorway to the right allows one to proceed up a spiral stairwell. In the ceiling above is the murder hole, which allowed for any potential assailants within the confined space of the lobby area to be subjected to a counterattack.

③ Ground-floor chamber

The doorway straight ahead allows access to the main chamber on the ground floor of the tower house. This chamber could have served as a cellar, or alternatively as space to accommodate servants or more junior members of the household. The wooden floor above was supported by the stone corbels that you see projecting from the east and west walls. Exposed bedrock can be seen in the southern end of the room. Proceeding up a flight of steps over this bedrock, the remains of brick-lined niches can be seen. These served as shelves when the chamber was used as a wine cellar in the eighteenth or nineteenth century. A passage in the east wall allows access to a large window embrasure that serves a round-arched window and a gun loop. The wooden stairs placed along the west wall facilitates access for visitors to the upper floors.

④ The 'Great Hall'

The top of this modern stairs provides a good vantage point to view the first-floor chamber known as the 'Great Hall'. As in many other tower houses, the room at this level is vaulted. Traces of wicker mats can be seen in the surface of the vault where the plasterwork is falling away. These mats were used in the construction of the vault – a technique called wickerwork centring (see p. 57). Placed centrally in the east wall is an early seventeenth-century fireplace with a classical surround – one of the earliest examples of neoclassical design in the area inspired by the ideals of the Renaissance. Turning away from this room, visitors proceed through a brick-lined window embrasure that has been breached in modern times to allow access into the ground-floor chamber of the earlier tower, known as the 'Earl's Bedroom'.

⑤ The 'Earl's Bedroom'

This room possesses a projecting window of seventeenth-century date, known as an oriel window. Unlike the smaller windows and loops evident in the room, the oriel window provided a grand vista of the castle's surroundings, and probably facilitated the enjoyment of gardens below, which were laid out in a symmetrical fashion much in vogue at the time. In the west wall, a window embrasure has been made into a fireplace. A now disappeared fire-hood (note the slot for a lintel that once would have supported it) would have directed smoke through the window opening. Entering a doorway in the east wall of the 'Earl's Bedroom', one passes through the original entry lobby of the early tower before reaching the base of another spiral stairwell known as the 'black stairs'.

⑥ The 'black stairs'

This stairwell is much narrower and rougher in construction than the spiral stairwell in the later tower block. As the stairwell proceeds upwards, note the blocked window loops that once provided a view to the south-east before the extension of the castle. A flat-headed doorway off this stairwell allows access to a narrow passage that widens into a small garderobe (toilet chamber). Further up the stairwell, an arched doorway allows entry into the first-floor chamber. This room is known as the 'Young Ladies Bedroom'.

⑦ The 'Young Ladies' Bedroom' and the 'Priest's Room' ⑧

The floor of this room has been partially removed, revealing the top of the stone vault that covers the 'Earl's Bedroom' below. The window embrasure in the west wall possesses a timber sill that appears to be original (that is, late fifteenth-century). A window in the east wall is now blocked, though it once would have looked out onto the earlier bawn before the extension of the castle. A doorway in the south-east allows access into a passage that links the 'Young Ladies' Bedroom' with the 'Family Room' on the second floor of the later tower block. Going back up the spiral stairwell, another arched doorway allows access into the second-floor chamber – the 'Priest's Room'. Like the 'Earl's Bedchamber', this room is vaulted. Note the corbels projecting from the walls that would have supported a timber floor.

⑨ The 'Kitchen'

Continuing further up the spiral stairs, an arched doorway opens onto the uppermost floor in the early tower. Originally, the third floor would have contained the hall, as is evident from the larger, more ornate windows – the examples in the north and south walls have ogee heads. With the building of the extension, this room ceased to be used as the hall, and was reutilized as the 'kitchen'. This room was now provided with a large fireplace, along with a smaller one to the side, both of which are served by a large chimneystack with a distinctive funnel shape. The presence of an inbuilt kitchen is quite unusual in tower houses. The east wall of the 'kitchen' has been largely quarried away and a thin partition wall with an arched doorway allows access to the 'Chapel' on the fourth floor of the later extension.

⑩ The battlements and the 'Blarney Stone'

Continuing up the stairwell, the visitor finally reaches the battlemented parapets with its narrow wall-walk. Along the western and southern length of the parapets of the early tower, the battlements project outwards from the façade of the building – this feature is known by specialists as machicolation. Closer inspection of the chimneystack at parapet level reveals it to have been rebuilt at some stage, most likely in the early seventeenth century. A flight of steps allows access onto the battlemented parapets of the later tower block. Proceeding onto the larger block of the castle, visitors make their way on a narrow wall-walk that is floored by flagstones set at an angle to allow for the dispersal of rainwater through drains at the foot of the parapet walls. In an effort to waterproof the wall-walk, the side joints between these sloped flagstones are covered with capstones. The battlements, again called machicolation, project outwards. Gaps in the floor by the parapet wall would have allowed objects to be thrown down on any would-be attackers trying to besiege the castle below. The 'Blarney Stone' is located at the base of the machicolation in the south wall – the stone is famed for bequeathing the gift of beguiling or cajoling speech if one kisses it! On the eastern battlements, there is a round-arched bell-cote. A turret in the north-east corner contains a stairwell that allows access to the floor below – the 'Chapel'.

⑪ The 'Chapel'

This is the principal chamber at fourth-floor level, called the 'Chapel', presumably due to the pointed window embrasures that give it a religious appearance. Unlike the principal chambers below, the 'Chapel' occupies the complete floor area at this level. This is characteristic of many tower houses in the south and west of Ireland, where the floor levels are divided into a principal and ancillary chamber except for the uppermost floor. Access to the 'kitchen' is via an arched doorway in one side of a window embrasure at the north end of the room. This doorway is not an original feature and was most likely inserted in post-medieval times. Two wall presses, each with a pointed segmental arch, are located in the corners at the south end of the 'Chapel'. Like the principal chambers below, this room is lit by square-hooded windows that were inserted sometime in the late sixteenth or early seventeenth century, though in the north wall the original window is still preserved – an ogee-headed example, typically fifteenth to sixteenth century in date.

⑫ Spiral stairs and Garderobe chamber ⑬

Proceeding down the main stairwell, with its carved limestone steps polished from centuries of use, one approaches an arched doorway opening off the stairwell. This allows access, via a short corridor, to the 'Banqueting Hall'. Before emerging into the main chamber, on the right-hand side, a short flight of steps leads to small dark room that was used as a garderobe or toilet chamber. Like other small chambers in the north end of the castle, the corner of the stairwell block associated with the earlier tower projects into this room. A latrine chute can be seen in the floor in one corner of the chamber, whose outlet is located in the north façade between the second- and third-floor levels. A slight instep and a pair of joist-holes in the north wall above this chute suggest the original presence of a wooden latrine seat. In the south wall at another corner of the room is a wall press. Like most of the other small chambers in the castle, the room has a pointed barrel vault with traces of wickerwork centring.

⑭ The 'Banqueting Hall'

In the 'Banqueting Hall' itself, there are the remains of a fireplace (now blocked) in the east wall, surmounted by a modern timber lintel. Only the sides of the fireplace surround survive. Like the other principal chambers in the castle, the room is provided with a number of large windows. These are later insertions, as evidenced by the stone surrounds of earlier openings visible in the exterior below two of them. Intriguingly, there is a pointed arch with traces of wicker centring projecting slightly from the north wall. Its appearance initially is rather puzzling – was this chamber originally vaulted? On closer inspection, the shadow of the vault in the south wall is revealed, indicating that the room was indeed vaulted when first built. The presence of a second vault follows a pattern commonly found in Munster, where many tower houses were vaulted at both first- and third-floor levels. The fireplace, probably of comparable date to the early seventeenth-century classical fireplace below in the 'Great Hall', was clearly inserted after the removal of the vault.

⑮ Ancillary chamber

Going back down the stairwell with its finely carved steps, an arched doorway allows entry directly into an ancillary chamber. The corner of the stairwell block associated with the earlier tower projects into the far end of this room. A corner window-loop, which formerly lit the stairwell of the first tower, is still evident. Its opening remains unblocked, allowing occupants within this ancillary chamber a view into the stairwell, the 'black stairs', as it rises through the older tower. Underneath the sill of the single window in this room is a slop-hole that allowed for the disposal of waste water. The room possesses a pointed barrel vault, well-covered with plaster, but with traces of wickerwork centring still evident.

⑯ The 'Family Room'

The principal room on the second floor, the 'Family Room', is accessed down the spiral stairwell via an arched doorway. After entering this doorway, one proceeds along a short corridor, at the end of which is an inserted brick-lined doorway, which replaced an earlier doorway just to the north of it. This allows access into a rather large room, dominated by a massive fireplace, which extends across the whole length of the north wall. This fireplace was blocked and replaced with a narrower one. A wall press with a segmental arch is located in the east wall at the south-east corner. There are large windows in the east, south and west walls of this room, typically two- to three-light windows crowned with square hood-moulding on the exterior. These windows replaced earlier openings – visible below the exterior of the windows are the stone sills of earlier single-light openings. They were in all probability ogee-headed windows similar in appearance to the surviving example in the west wall. Beside this ogee-headed window, there is an arched doorway, which allows access, via a short flight of steps, down into a mural corridor. This passage facilitates entry into the first-floor chamber of the earlier tower, the 'Young Ladies' Bedroom'.

⑰–⑲ Smaller chambers and exit

Further down the spiral stairwell, the observer comes upon another arched doorway. This allows entry into a dogleg corridor, lit by a small flat-headed ope as it turns the corner, via a flight of steps, towards a small chamber that acted as a garderobe or toilet chamber. A latrine chute can be seen in the floor along the north side of the chamber, whose outlet is located in the exterior of the same wall at first-floor level. Located in the south wall at the south-west corner is a wall press. The room possesses a pointed barrel vault with traces of wicker centring. Again, the corner of the earlier tower can be seen projecting into this room.

Continuing down the stairwell, the visitor encounters another arched doorway that allows access into a mural corridor in the thickness of the north wall. The entrance into the earlier tower was originally located at the end of this corridor.

When the tower house was being extended in the sixteenth century, it was decided to block this entrance and insert a flat-headed doorway in the north wall of the corridor to allow access to the 'black stairs' of the earlier tower. Beyond this doorway is a short flight of steps that connects with the stairwell in the earlier tower. Why they blocked an existing entrance and went to the trouble of mining through a wall of massive proportions is not clear, though it could be argued that it created a greater degree of privacy or seclusion for the 'Earl's Bedroom', the chamber on the ground floor of the earlier tower.

Down the stairwell again, the observer encounters an arched doorway that allows access into a short corridor built into the thickness of the east wall – this is the original entrance into the 'Great Hall'. The corridor terminates in a large window embrasure that has been widened to facilitate the insertion of a two-light, square-hooded, mullioned window. On the floor of this embrasure is the murder-hole that originally allowed the lobby area below to be covered by deadly fire in case the entrance was breached. This embrasure effectively acted as an antechamber for the principal chamber at first-floor level and, once through the antechamber, visitors are confronted with the large vaulted space of the 'Great Hall'.

Descending the stairs once more finally brings visitors back to the entrance lobby. While initially confusing to the modern eye, with its myriad passages, stairs and rooms, for a couple of hundred years Blarney Castle provided a home that signalled the authority and social standing of one of the most prominent noble families in Ireland – the MacCarthys, lords of Muskerry.

Notes

Chapter 1. The MacCarthys, lords of Muskerry: their historical pedigree

1 Donnchadh Ó Corráin, *Ireland before the Normans* (Dublin, 1972), p. 152.

2 W.F. Butler, 'The barony of Muskerry', *Journal of the Cork Historical and Archaeological Society*, 16 (1910), 81–8, 120–7 at 120; Diarmuid Ó Murchadha, *Family names of County Cork* (Cork, 1996), pp 49–50.

3 F.X. Martin, 'The Normans: arrival and settlement, 1169–c.1300' in T.W. Moody & F.X. Martin (eds), *The course of Irish history* (Dublin, 2001), pp 95–112.

4 Ó Murchadha, *Family names*, pp 50–1.

5 For an excellent overview of this period in Cork's history, consult A.F. O'Brien, 'Politics, economy and society: the development of Cork and the Irish south-coast region, c.1170 to c.1583' in Patrick O'Flanagan & Cornelius G. Buttimer (eds), *Cork, history and society: interdisciplinary essays on the history of an Irish county* (Dublin, 1993), pp 83–156.

6 For more in-depth discussion on the expansion of the Muskerry lordship, see Kenneth Nicholls, 'The development of lordship in County Cork' in O'Flanagan & Buttimer (eds), *Cork, history and society*, pp 157–211 at pp 172–6.

7 Nicholas Canny, *From reformation to restoration: Ireland, 1534–1660* (Dublin, 1987), pp 1–3.

8 Nicholas Canny, 'Early modern Ireland, c.1500–1700' in R.F. Foster (ed.), *The Oxford illustrated history of Ireland* (Oxford, 1989), pp 104–60 at pp 104–5.

9 David Edwards, *The Ormond lordship in County Kilkenny, 1515–1642: the rise and fall of Butler feudal power* (Dublin, 2003), pp 20, 61.

10 Katharine Simms, *From kings to warlords: the changing political structure of Gaelic Ireland in the later Middle Ages* (Woodbridge & Wolfeboro, 1987), pp 19–20.

11 Simms, *Kings to warlords*, p. 39.

12 Butler, 'Barony of Muskerry', 122–3; Rolf Loeber, 'An architectural history of Gaelic castles and settlements, 1370–1600' in Patrick J. Duffy, David Edwards & Elizabeth FitzPatrick (eds), *Gaelic Ireland: land, lordship and settlement, c.1250–c.1650* (Dublin, 2001), pp 271–314 at p. 280.

13 John T. Collins, 'The McCarthys of Muskerry and Blarney Castle', *Old Blarney: Journal of the Blarney and District Historical Society*, 4 (1999), 11–27 at 11.

14 Samuel Lewis, *A topographical dictionary of Ireland*, 2 vols (London, 1837; repr. New York, 1970), i, p. 211.

15 Mark Bence-Jones, *A guide to Irish country houses* (London, 1988), p. 43; Brian de Breffny & George Mott, *Castles of Ireland* (London, 1977), p. 54; James N. Healy, *The castles of County Cork* (Cork, 1988), p. 21.

16   Butler, 'Barony of Muskerry', 123; Cecil Crawford Woods, 'Blarney Castle, County Cork, double structure of its keep', *Journal of the Cork Historical and Archaeological Society*, 2 (1896), 337–44 at 344; Healy, *Castles of County Cork*, p. 21.

17   Nicholls, 'Development of lordship', p. 173.

18   Ibid., p. 173.

19   Hanneke Ronnes, *Architecture and elite culture in the United Provinces, England and Ireland, 1500–1700* (Amsterdam, 2006), pp 129–30; ibid., 'Continental traces at Carrick-on-Suir and contemporary Irish castles: a preliminary study of date-and-initial stones' in Thomas Herron and Michael Potterton (eds), *Ireland in the Renaissance, c.1540–1660* (Dublin, 2007), pp 255–73.

20   Mike Salter, *The castles of Munster* (Malvern, 2004), p. 28.

21   David Sweetman, *Medieval castles of Ireland* (Cork, 1999), p. 163; Salter, *Castles of Munster*, p. 28; Nicholls, 'Lordship in County Cork', p. 173.

22   Nicholls, 'Lordship in County Cork', p. 174.

23   Butler, 'Barony of Muskerry', 124; Healy, *Castles of County Cork*, p. 21; Herbert Webb Gillman, 'Carrignamuck Castle, County Cork: a stronghold of the MacCarthys', *Journal of the Cork Historical and Archaeological Society*, 1 (1892), 11–19, 30–7 at 18.

24   Rolf Loeber, *The geography and practice of English colonization in Ireland from 1534 to 1609* (Athlone, 1991), p. 8.

25   Canny, *From reformation to restoration*, pp 1–2; G.A. Hayes-McCoy, 'The Tudor conquest (1534–1603)' in Moody & Martin (eds), *The course of Irish history*, pp 139–51 at pp 140–1; James F. Lydon, *The making of Ireland, from ancient times to the present* (London & New York, 1998), pp 126–8.

26   Canny, *From reformation to restoration*, p. 41; Hayes-McCoy, 'Tudor conquest', pp 141–4; Lydon, *Making of Ireland*, pp 137–8.

27   Nicholas Canny, *Kingdom and colony, Ireland in the Atlantic world, 1560–1800* (Baltimore & London, 1988), pp 31–2.

28   Canny, *From reformation to restoration*, pp 43–4; ibid., 'Early modern Ireland', pp 105–6; Lydon, *Making of Ireland*, pp 135–6.

29   Thomas Crofton Croker, *Researches in the south of Ireland* (London, 1824), p. 294.

30   Butler, 'Barony of Muskerry', 126; John T. Collins, 'Some McCarthys of Blarney and Ballea', *Journal of the Cork Historical and Archaeological Society*, 59 (1954), 1–10, 82–8 at 1–2; Healy, *Castles of County Cork*, p. 21; Ó Murchadha, *Family names*, p. 59; Webb Gillman, 'Carrignamuck Castle', 31.

31   Loeber, *English colonization*, p. 48.

32   Butler, 'Barony of Muskerry', 126; Healy, *Castles of County Cork*, p. 21; Herbert Webb Gillman, 'Sir Cormac McTeige MacCarthy and the sept lands of Muskerry, Co. Cork; with a historical pedigree', *Journal of the Cork Historical and Archaeological Society*, 1 (1892), 193–200 at 195.

33   Crofton Croker, *Researches*, p. 294; Webb Gillman, 'Carrignamuck Castle', 32.

34   Collins, 'McCarthys of Muskerry', 16; Ó Murchadha, *Family names*, p. 59.

35   Webb Gillman, 'Carrignamuck Castle', 33; ibid., 'Sir Cormac McTeige MacCarthy', 199.

36 Collins, 'McCarthys of Blarney and Ballea', 5.

37 Ó Murchadha, *Family names*, p. 59.

38 Standish O'Grady (ed.), *Pacata Hibernia or history of the wars in Ireland during the reign of Queen Elizabeth*, 2 vols (London, 1896), i, p. 299.

39 J.A. Simpson & E.S.C. Weiner, *The Oxford English dictionary*, 20 vols (2nd ed. Oxford, 1989), ii, p. 263.

40 De Breffny & Mott, *Castles of Ireland*, p. 54; Healy, *Castles of County Cork*, pp 21–3.

41 Crofton Croker, *Researches*, p. 306.

42 Francis S. Mahony, *The reliques of Father Prout* (London, 1860), pp 55–62, quoted in Robert E. Connolly, *If walls could talk: great Irish castles tell their stories* (Dublin, 2004), p. 182; de Breffny & Mott, *Castles of Ireland*, p. 54

43 Collins, 'McCarthys of Muskerry', 21; Healy, *Castles of County Cork*, p. 23; Ó Murchadha, *Family names*, p. 60.

44 Collins, 'McCarthys of Muskerry', 21; Denise Maher, *Kilcrea Friary: Franciscan heritage in County Cork* (Cork, 1999), p. 35; Ó Murchadha, *Family names*, p. 60; Webb Gillman, 'Carrignamuck Castle', 35.

45 David B. Quinn, 'The Munster Plantation: problems and opportunities', *Journal of the Cork Historical and Archaeological Society*, 71 (1966), 19–40 at 35, 38.

46 Michael MacCarthy-Morrogh, *The Munster Plantation, English migration to southern Ireland, 1583–1641* (Oxford, 1986), p. 175.

47 Collins, 'McCarthys of Blarney and Ballea', 85; Collins, 'McCarthys of Muskerry', 21; Healy, *Castles of County Cork*, p. 23.

48 Collins, 'McCarthys of Blarney and Ballea', 85; Collins, 'McCarthys of Muskerry', 21.

49 Collins, 'McCarthys of Blarney and Ballea', 86.

50 Ibid.

51 Ibid.

52 Ibid.

53 Ibid.; Collins, 'McCarthys of Muskerry', 23; Healy, *Castles of County Cork*, p. 23; Ó Murchadha, *Family names*, p. 60.

54 R.C. Simington (ed.), *The Civil Survey, AD1654–1656: County of Waterford with appendices: Muskerry Barony, Co. Cork …* (Dublin, 1942), p. 375.

55 Collins, 'McCarthys of Blarney and Ballea', 86–8.

56 John A. Murphy, 'Cork: anatomy and essence' in O'Flanagan & Buttimer, (eds), *Cork, history and society*, pp 1–14 at p. 6.

57 Collins, 'McCarthys of Blarney and Ballea', 88; Healy, *Castles of County Cork*, p. 24; Ó Murchadha, *Family names*, p. 60.

58 William P. McCarthy, 'The litigious earl', *Journal of the Cork Historical and Archaeological Society*, 70 (1965), 7–13 at 8.

59 John T. Collins, 'Some McCarthys of Blarney and Ballea', *Journal of the Cork Historical and Archaeological Society*, 60 (1955), 1–5, 75–9 at 1; Webb Gillman, 'Carrignamuck Castle', 37.

60 McCarthy, 'Litigious earl', 8.

61 Collins, 'Some McCarthys of Blarney and Ballea', 1.

62 McCarthy 'Litigious earl', 9.

63 Collins, 'Some McCarthys of Blarney and Ballea', 3; ibid., 'McCarthys of Muskerry', 24; Healy, *Castles of County Cork*, p. 24.

64 C.J.F. McCarthy, 'An antiquary's note book, 12', *Journal of the Cork Historical and Archaeological Society*, 95 (1990), 158–64 at 164, fn 1.

65 McCarthy, 'Antiquary's notebook', 164; John Mulcahy, 'The Church of Ireland in Blarney', *Old Blarney: Journal of the Blarney and District Historical Society*, 3 (1993), 42–54 at 45.

66 Collins, 'McCarthys of Muskerry', 24–5; de Breffny & Mott, *Castles of Ireland*, p. 54; Healy, *Castles of County Cork*, p. 24.

67 Webb Gillman, 'Carrignamuck Castle', 37.

68 Collins, 'Some MacCarthys of Blarney and Ballea', 76.

69 De Breffny & Mott, *Castles of Ireland*, p. 54; McCarthy, 'Antiquary's notebook', 162.

70 Collins, 'Some MacCarthys of Blarney and Ballea', 76.

71 Ibid.

72 Mulcahy, 'Church of Ireland in Blarney', 45.

73 Collins, 'Some MacCarthys of Blarney and Ballea', 76–7; ibid., 'The McCarthys of Muskerry', 26–7; de Breffny & Mott, *Castles of Ireland*, p. 54; Healy, *Castles of County Cork*, p. 24.

74 Lydon, *Making of Ireland*, p.166.

75 Though according to de Breffny & Mott, *Castles of Ireland*, p. 54, this individual was still maintained as a tenant by the company until it was sold on to Sir Richard Pyne in 1703.

76 Mulcahy, 'Church of Ireland in Blarney', 45.

77 John Mulcahy, 'The diplomatic career of Captain James Jefferyes, Blarney Castle', *Old Blarney: Journal of the Blarney and District Historical Society*, 6 (2002), 7–30 at 8; M.G., 'Notes and queries', *Journal of the Cork Historical and Archaeological Society*, 17 (1911), 35–6 at 35; J.C., 'Notes and queries', *Journal of the Cork Historical and Archaeological Society*, 20 (1914), 156–8 at 156.

78 J.C., 'Notes and queries', 156.

79 Ibid., 156–7.

80 Ibid., 157–8.

81 Crofton Croker, *Researches*, p. 292; Lewis, *Topographical dictionary*, i, p. 211.

82 The drawing is published in Peter Harbison (ed.), *Beranger's views of Ireland* (Dublin, 1991), p. 44.

83 Charles Smith, *The ancient and present state of the county and city of Cork…* (Cork, 1750, 1893 ed.), p. 153.

84 Arthur Young, *A tour in Ireland with general observations on the present state of that kingdom made in the years 1776, 1777 and 1778* (repr. Cambridge, 1925), p. 103.

85 Michael Quane, 'Tour in Ireland by John Harden in 1797', *Journal of the Cork Historical and Archaeological Society*, 60 (1955), 80–7 at 83.

86 J.C., 'Notes and queries', 157–8.

87 Ibid., 158.

88 Colman O'Mahony, 'Bygone industries of Blarney and Dripsey', *Journal of Cork Historical and Archaeological Society*, 89 (1984), 77–87 at 87.

89 Ibid., 77; Young, *Tour in Ireland*, p. 102.

90 Ibid., p. 103.

91 Patrick O'Flanagan, 'Three hundred years of urban life: villages and towns in County Cork, *c.*1600 to 1901' in O'Flanagan & Buttimer (eds), *Cork, history and society*, pp 391–467 at p. 416.

92 Crofton Croker, *Researches*, p. 291.

93 Maura Cronin, 'Work and workers in Cork city and county, 1800–1900' in O'Flanagan & Buttimer (eds), *Cork, history and society*, pp 721–58 at p. 740; O'Mahony, 'Bygone industries', 84–6.

94 Crofton Croker, *Researches*, p. 306.

95 Bence-Jones, *Irish country houses*, p. 43.

96 B. Rooney, 'The Irish Exhibition at Olympia, 1888', *Irish Architectural and Decorative Studies*, 1 (1998), 101–19 at 109 n. 18; Neil Harris, 'Selling national culture: Ireland at the World's Columbian Exposition' in T.J. Edelstein (ed.), *Imagining an Irish past: the Celtic Revival, 1840–1940* (Chicago, 1992), pp 82–105 at p. 93, pls 40 & 41.

Chapter 2. Irish tower houses in context

1 Victor Chinnery, 'Barryscourt refurbished, the reinstatement of a late sixteenth-century Irish domestic interior' in Ludlow & Jameson (eds), *Barryscourt lectures* (Kinsale, Cork, 2004), pp 177–224 at p. 190.

2 Harold G. Leask, *Irish castles and castellated houses* (Dundalk, 1951), p. 153.

3 Terry Barry, 'Rural settlement in medieval Ireland' in Terry Barry (ed.), *A history of settlement in Ireland* (London & New York, 2000), pp 110–23 at p. 119; ibid., 'The study of medieval Irish castles: a bibliographic survey', *Proceedings of the Royal Irish Academy*, 108 (2008), 115–36 at 129.

4 Tadhg O'Keeffe, *Medieval Ireland: an archaeology* (Stroud, 2000), p. 34.

5 Colm J. Donnelly, 'Tower houses and late medieval secular settlement in county Limerick' in Duffy, Edwards & FitzPatrick (eds), *Gaelic Ireland*, pp 315–28 at pp 319–21.

6 O'Keeffe, *Medieval Ireland*, p. 53.

7 T.J. Westropp, 'The ancient castles of the County of Limerick', *Proceedings of the Royal Irish Academy*, 26C (1907), 55–108 at 70–1.

8 C. Ó Danachair, 'Irish tower houses and their regional distribution', *Bealoideas*, 45–7 (1977–9), 158–63 at 160.

9 O'Keeffe, *Medieval Ireland*, p. 51.

10 Leask, *Irish castles*, pp 76–7. In fact, this legislation was first passed in Co. Louth in 1428, and thereafter extended to the rest of the Pale in 1430 (and not 1429, as often quoted). Leask mistakenly dated the statute 8 Henry VI to 1429, thereby leading many scholars astray, only to be corrected more recently: see John Bradley & Ben Murtagh, 'Brady's Castle, Thomastown, Co. Kilkenny: a 14th-century fortified town

house' in John R. Kenyon & Kieran O'Conor (eds), *The medieval castle in Ireland and Wales* (Dublin, 2003), pp 194–216 at pp 211–12.

11 Tom McNeill, *Castles in Ireland, feudal power in a Gaelic World* (London & New York, 1997), p. 202; O'Keeffe, *Medieval Ireland*, p. 51.

12 Bradley & Murtagh, 'Brady's Castle', p. 214; McNeill, *Castles in Ireland*, p. 203.

13 Terry Barry, 'The archaeology of the tower house in late medieval Ireland' in Hans Andersson and Jes Wienberg (eds), *The study of medieval archaeology, Lund Studies in Medieval Archaeology 13* (Stockholm, 1993), pp 211–17 at pp 214–15; McNeill, *Castles in Ireland*, p. 203; Bradley & Murtagh, 'Brady's Castle', p. 215.

14 McNeill, *Castles in Ireland*, p. 203; O'Keeffe, *Medieval Ireland*, p. 51.

15 O'Keeffe *Medieval Ireland*, p. 52.

16 Ibid., p. 53; Sweetman, *Medieval castles*, p. 137; David Sweetman, 'The origin and development of the tower house in Ireland' in Ludlow & Jameson (eds), *Barryscourt lectures*, pp 261–87 at p. 267.

17 O'Keeffe, *Medieval Ireland*, p. 53.

18 Maurice Craig, *The architecture of Ireland from the earliest times to 1880* (Portrane, 1989), p. 97; Leask, *Irish castles*, p. 79–88; McNeill, *Castles in Ireland*, p. 201; O'Keeffe, *Medieval Ireland*, p. 47; Sweetman, *Medieval castles*, pp 138–9.

19 Standish O'Grady, *Caithreim Thoirdelbhaigh*, 2 vols (Dublin, 1929), ii, p. 29; Joep Leerssen, *Mere Irish and Fior Ghael: studies in the idea of Irish nationality, its development and literary expression prior to the nineteenth century* (Amsterdam & Philadelphia, 1986), p. 200.

20 McNeill, *Castles in Ireland*, p. 222.

21 Ross Samson, 'The rise and fall of tower houses in post-Reformation Scotland' in Ross Samson (ed.), *The social archaeology of houses* (Edinburgh, 1990), pp 197–243 at p. 207.

22 Mary O'Dowd, 'Gaelic economy and society' in Ciaran Brady & Raymond Gillespie (eds), *Natives and newcomers, the making of Irish colonial society, 1534–1641* (Dublin, 1986), pp 120–47 at pp 120–1.

23 Chinnery, 'Barryscourt refurbished', p. 187.

24 Edward MacLysaght, *Irish life in the seventeenth century* (Shannon, 1969), p. 15.

25 Tadhg O'Keeffe, 'Barryscourt castle and the Irish tower-house' in Ludlow & Jameson (eds), *Barryscourt lectures*, pp 3–31 at p. 10.

26 M.W. Thompson, *The decline of the castle* (Cambridge, 1987), p. 26.

27 Samson, 'The rise and fall of tower-houses', p. 207.

28 O'Keeffe, 'Barryscourt castle', p. 26.

29 Matthew Johnson, *Behind the castle gate, from medieval to renaissance* (London & New York, 2002), pp 68–9.

30 Johnson, *Behind the castle gate*, p. 69.

31 Johnson, *Behind the castle gate*, p. 12.

32 Tadhg O'Keeffe, 'Space, place, habitus: geographies of practice in an Anglo-Norman manor' in Howard B. Clarke, Jacinta Prunty & Mark Hennessy (eds), *Surveying Ireland's past: multidisciplinary essays in honour of Anngret Simms* (Dublin, 2004), pp 73–98 at p. 89.

33 Brian de Breffny & Rosemary ffolliott, *The houses of Ireland* (London, 1975), p. 52; Leask, *Irish castles*, p. 104.

34 Craig, *Architecture of Ireland*, p. 109.

35 H.G. Leask, 'Early seventeenth-century houses in Ireland' in E.M. Jope (ed.), *Studies in building history: essays in recognition of the work of B.H. St John O'Neil* (London, 1961), pp 243–50 at p. 244.

36 Toby Barnard, *Making the grand figure, lives and possessions in Ireland, 1641–1770* (New Haven & London, 2004), pp 26, 189, fig. 49.

Chapter 3. *The layout and use of Blarney Castle*

1 Loeber, 'Gaelic castles and settlements', pp 271–314 at pp 304–5.

2 Catherine Marie O'Sullivan, *Hospitality in medieval Ireland, 900–1500* (Dublin, 2004), p. 65.

3 Chinnery, 'Barryscourt refurbished', pp 177–224 at p. 195.

4 John O'Donovan (ed.), *Annals of the kingdom of Ireland by the Four Masters, from the earliest period to the year 1616*, 7 vols (Dublin, 1856, repr. Dublin, 1990), v, p. 1799.

5 Johnson, *Behind the castle gate*, p. 38.

6 Dave Pollock, 'The bawn exposed: recent excavations at Barryscourt' in Ludlow & Jameson (eds), *Barryscourt lectures*, pp 145–75; ibid., 'The Barryscourt hall and the remains of some other medieval timber buildings' in Conleth Manning (ed.), *From ringforts to fortified houses: studies on castles and other monuments in honour of David Sweetman* (Bray, 2007), pp 261–72 at pp 261–6.

7 Simington (ed.), *Civil Survey*, vol. vi, p. 375.

8 Terry Barry, 'Harold Leask's "single towers": Irish tower houses as part of larger settlement complexes', *Château Gaillard*, 22 (2006), 27–33 at 30.

9 Quane, 'Tour in Ireland', pl. ix.

10 Standish O'Grady (ed.), *Pacata Hibernia or history of the wars in Ireland during the reign of Queen Elizabeth*, 2 vols (London, 1896), ii, p. 227. The *Pacata Hibernia*, a contemporary account of the Nine Years War, suggests a more extensive complex than survives today. The same source describes in further detail a curtain wall, to which the main keep was attached on the north side, 18ft wide in places and with a guard tower at each corner. It is noteworthy that Blarney Castle was never attacked during the course of the sixteenth century.

11 Colin Breen, *The Gaelic lordship of the O'Sullivan Beare* (Dublin, 2005), pp 154–5.

12 Tom Williamson, *Polite landscapes, gardens and society in eighteenth-century England* (Baltimore, 1995), pp 32–3.

13 Brooke S. Blades, 'English villages in the Londonderry plantation', *Post-medieval Archaeology*, 20 (1986), 257–69 at 261, fig. 2.

14 Niall McCullough, *Palimpsest, change in the Irish building tradition* (Dublin, 1994), p. 60.

15 De Breffny & ffolliott, *Houses of Ireland*, p. 74.

16 Pollock, 'The bawn exposed', pp 167–72.

17 Eric Klingelhöfer, 'Edmund Spenser at Kilcolman Castle: the archaeological evidence', *Post-Medieval Archaeology*, 39:1 (2005), 133–54 at 143–4.

18 Anon., 'Proceedings', *Journal of the Royal Society of Antiquaries of Ireland*, 23 (1893), 329–43 at 340; Mark Samuel & Kate Hamlyn, *Blarney Castle: its history, development and purpose* (Cork, 2007), p. 92.

19 Simington (ed.), *Civil Survey*, vol. vi, p. 375.

20 Denis Power with Elizabeth Byrne, Ursula Egan, Sheila Lane & Mary Sleeman, *Archaeological inventory of County Cork. Vol. 2: east and south Cork* (Dublin, 1994), pp 218–19, ibid., *Archaeological inventory of County Cork. Vol. 4: north Cork, part 2* (Dublin, 2000), pp 523–3; Olive Alcock, Kathy de hÓra and Paul Gosling, *Archaeological inventory of County Galway. Vol. 2: north Galway* (Dublin, 1999), pp 404–5.

21 This lintel, with its ogee profiles and recessed spandrels, is within a portion of the north façade that preserves a stretch of the original bawn constructed by Cormac 'Láidir' mac Taidhg in the 1480s. Such a window would have lit the interior of an ancillary building such as a hall inside the courtyard area before the castle was extended.

22 Rolf Loeber, 'Early classicism in Ireland: architecture before the Georgian era', *Architectural History*, 22 (1979), 49–63 at 54.

23 Loeber, 'Early classicism in Ireland', 52.

24 Ibid., 50.

25 Ibid., 50–1.

26 Ibid., 51.

27 Ibid., 52–4.

28 Crawford Woods, 'Blarney Castle', 338, 343.

29 Ibid., 343.

30 Quane, 'Tour in Ireland', 83; Charles Mosley (ed.), *Burke's peerage & baronetage*, 2 vols (106th ed. London, 1999), i, p. 634.

31 O'Keeffe, *Medieval Ireland*, pp 53–5.

32 Leask, *Irish castles*, p. 91.

33 Chinnery, 'Barryscourt refurbished', p. 196.

34 Karena Morton, 'Irish medieval wall painting' in Ludlow & Jameson (eds), *Barryscourt lectures*, pp 313–49 at p. 318; Con Manning, pers. comm., 23 June 2011.

35 Jane Fenlon, *Goods & chattels: a survey of early household inventories in Ireland* (Dublin, 2003).

36 De Breffny & ffolliott, *Houses of Ireland*, p. 34.

37 O'Sullivan, *Hospitality in medieval Ireland*, pp 99–100; Katharine Simms, 'Native sources for Gaelic settlement: the house poems' in Duffy, Edwards & FitzPatrick (eds), *Gaelic Ireland*, pp 246–67 at p. 247.

38 Leask, *Irish castles*, pp 92, 124.

39 Fenlon, *Goods & chattels*, p. 4.

40 W. Fitzgerald, 'Notes on Sir John MacCoghlan, Knight of Cloghan, Chief of Delvin-MacCoghlan who died in 1590', *Journal of the Royal Society of Antiquaries of Ireland*, 43 (1913), 223–31 at 230.

41 Ibid., p. 228; O'Donovan (ed.), *Annals of the Four Masters*, vi, p. 1893.

42 Chinnery, 'Barryscourt refurbished', pp 208–9.

43 Rory Sherlock, 'Cross-cultural occurrences of mutations in tower house architecture', *Journal of Irish Archaeology*, 15 (2006), 73–91 at 78.

44 Leask, *Irish castles*, pp 91–2.

45 Rory Sherlock, 'The evolution of the Irish tower house as a domestic space', *Proceedings of the Royal Irish Academy*, 111C (2010), 115–40 at 126.

46 A.G. Rutherford, 'A social interpretation of the castle in Scotland' (PhD, U. Glasgow, 1998), p. 4.

47 Samson, 'The rise and fall of tower houses', p. 206; Paula Henderson, 'Life at the top: sixteenth- and seventeenth-century roofscapes', *Country Life*, 177 (1985), 6–9 at 6.

48 Chinnery, 'Barryscourt refurbished', pp 200–1.

49 Crawford Woods, 'Blarney Castle', 340.

50 Ibid.

51 Ciaran Brady, 'Political women and reform in Tudor Ireland' in Margaret MacCurtain & Mary O'Dowd (eds), *Women in early modern Ireland* (Dublin, 1991), pp 69–90 at p. 70.

52 Elizabeth McKenna, 'Was there a political role for women in medieval Ireland?' in Christine Meek & Katharine Simms (eds), *The fragility of her sex? Medieval Irish women in their European context* (Dublin, 1996), pp 163–74 at p. 164.

53 Brady, 'Political women', pp 78–9.

54 Ibid., pp 87.

55 Mary McAuliffe, 'The lady in the tower, the social and political role of women in tower houses' in Meek & Simms (eds), *The fragility of her sex?*, pp 153–62 at p. 159; Kenneth Nicholls, 'Irishwomen and property in the sixteenth century' in MacCurtain & O'Dowd (eds), *Women in early modern Ireland*, pp 17–31 at p. 20.

56 Nicholls, 'Irishwomen and property', p. 25.

57 McAuliffe, 'Lady in the tower', p. 154; Rutherford, 'Castle in Scotland', p. 120.

58 Roberta Gilchrist, 'Ambivalent bodies: gender and medieval archaeology' in Jenny Moore & Eleanor Scott (eds), *Invisible people and processes: writing gender and childhood into European archaeology* (London & New York, 1997), pp 42–58 at p. 44; Tadhg O'Keeffe, 'Concepts of "castle" and the construction of identity in medieval and post-medieval Ireland', *Irish Geography*, 34:1 (2001), 69–88 at 79.

59 Roberta Gilchrist, *Gender and archaeology: contesting the past* (London & New York, 1999), p. 121; O'Keeffe, 'Concepts of "castle"', 77–8.

60 Brady, 'Political women', p. 70.

61 Leask, *Irish castles*, pp 91–2.

62 McAuliffe, 'Lady in the tower', p. 156.

Chapter 4. The 'transition' from castle to country house at Blarney

1 Simington (ed.), *Civil Survey*, vol. vi, p. 375.

2 E.M. Jope, 'Moyry, Charlemont, Castleraw and Richhill: fortification to architecture in the north of Ireland, 1570–1700', *Ulster Journal of Archaeology*, 23 (1960), 97–123

at 97; Craig, *Architecture of Ireland*, p. 122; P.M. Kerrigan, *Castles and fortifications in Ireland, 1485–1945* (Cork, 1995), pp 6, 65.

3   Craig, *Architecture of Ireland*, p. 133.

4   Sharon Weadick, 'How popular were fortified houses in Irish castle building history? A look at their numbers in the archaeological record and distribution patterns' in James Lyttleton and Colin Rynne (eds), *Plantation Ireland: settlement and material culture, c.1550–c.1700* (Dublin, 2009), pp 61–85 at p. 78.

5   Craig, *Architecture of Ireland*, p. 123.

6   T.C. Barnard, 'The political, material and mental culture of the Cork settlers, c.1650–1700' in O'Flanagan & Buttimer (eds), *Cork, history and society*, pp 309–65 at p. 323.

7   C.T. Cairns, *Irish tower houses: a Co. Tipperary case study* (Dublin, 1987), pp 17–18; McCullough, *Palimpsest*, p. 55; John O'Callaghan, 'Fortified houses of the sixteenth century in south Wexford', *Journal of the Old Wexford Society*, 8 (1980–1), 1–51.

8   Leask, *Irish castles*, p. 106; for plans of these sites see Sweetman, *Medieval castles*, pp 119, 160, 166, figs 96, 135, 140.

9   McNeill, *Castles in Ireland*, p. 221.

10   Loeber, 'Gaelic castles and settlements', pp 271–314 at p. 275; Thompson, *Decline of the castle*, p. 24.

11   Denis Power et al., *Archaeological inventory of County Cork. Vol. 3: Mid-Cork* (Dublin, 1997), p. 359.

12   Crawford Woods, 'Blarney Castle', 343.

13   Collins, 'MacCarthys of Blarney and Ballea', 86; McCarthy, 'Antiquary's notebook', 164, fn 1.

14   McCarthy, 'Antiquary's notebook', 164; Mulcahy, 'Church of Ireland in Blarney', 45.

15   According to one source, this mansion was built around 1745 (see Mosley (ed.), *Burke's Peerage*, i, p. 634). It has also been suggested that the seventeenth-century manor-house was gothicized and extended to the north, probably in the 1760s, following the marriage of James St John Jefferyes and Arabella Fitzgibbon in 1762 (see Frederick O'Dwyer, 'In search of Christopher Myers: pioneer of the Gothic revival in Ireland' in Michael McCarthy & Karina O'Neill (eds), *Studies in the Gothic Revival*, pp 51–111 at pp 87–8.

16   A third tower lies c.200m to the east of the 'Lookout tower', integrated into the east end of a later stable block. It is doubtful if this tower was integral to the bawn perimeter, given the substantial distance between it and the tower house, and the fact that it lacks defensive features. More than likely it was also designed as a folly.

17   James Howley, *The follies and garden buildings of Ireland* (New Haven & London, 1993), pp 1–2.

18   Ibid., p. 2.

19   Ibid.

20   Ibid.

21   Bence-Jones, *Irish country houses*, p. 43; Jeremy Williams, *A companion guide to architecture in Ireland, 1837–1921* (Dublin, 1994), p. 71.

Chapter 5. The chronology of Blarney Castle's development

1 A.J. Jordan, 'Date, chronology and evolution of the County Wexford tower house', *Journal of the Wexford Historical Society*, 13 (1990–1), 30–81.

2 Colm J. Donnelly, 'Sectionally constructed tower houses: a review of the evidence from County Limerick', *Journal of the Royal Society of Antiquaries of Ireland*, 128 (1998), 26–34 at 33.

3 Sherlock, 'Mutations in tower house architecture', 78.

4 Crawford Woods, 'Blarney Castle', 340. The same author went on to describe the interior of the castle, making the interesting observation that the original entrance into the earlier tower was in the east wall, ten feet above the level of the ground, opening into a passage linking 'the Earl's Bedroom' with 'the black stairs'; this same passage also appearing to bear indications of a murder-hole in its ceiling. The present survey largely concurs with this, though there is no evidence for a murder-hole in the same passage.

5 Salter, *Castles of Munster*, p. 28; Samuel & Hamlyn, *Blarney Castle*, pp 131–2.

6 Salter, *Castles of Munster*, p. 28–9; Samuel & Hamlyn, *Blarney Castle*, p. 132.

7 Healy, *Castles of County Cork*, p. 21.

8 Collins, 'McCarthys of Muskerry', 14.

9 Ibid., 21.

10 Elizabeth FitzPatrick & Paul Walsh, 'Buildings and architecture' in Elizabeth FitzPatrick, Madeline O'Brien & Paul Walsh (eds), *Archaeological investigations in Galway City, 1987–1998* (Bray, 2004), pp 337–55 at p. 349.

11 Samuel & Hamlyn, *Blarney Castle*, p. 128.

12 Ibid.

13 Ibid., pp 131–2.

14 Leask, *Irish castles*, p. 106.

15 Samuel & Hamlyn, *Blarney Castle*, pp 132–3; Quane, 'Tour in Ireland', 83.

Bibliography

Alcock, Olive, Kathy de hÓra and Paul Gosling, *Archaeological inventory of County Galway. Volume 2: North Galway* (Dublin, 1999).

Anon., 'Proceedings', *Journal of the Royal Society of Antiquaries of Ireland*, 23 (1893), 329–43.

Barnard, T.C., 'The political, material and mental culture of the Cork settlers, *c.*1650–1700' in O'Flanagan & Buttimer (eds), *Cork, history and society* (1993), pp 309–65.

— *Making the grand figure: lives and possessions in Ireland, 1641–1770* (New Haven & London, 2004).

Barry, Terry, 'The archaeology of the tower house in late medieval Ireland' in Hans Andersson and Jes Wienberg (eds), *The study of medieval archaeology, Lund Studies in Medieval Archaeology* 13 (Stockholm, 1993), pp 211–17.

— 'Rural settlement in medieval Ireland' in Terry Barry (ed.), *A history of settlement in Ireland* (London & New York, 2000), pp 110–23.

— 'Harold Leask's "single towers": Irish tower houses as part of larger settlement complexes', *Château Gaillard*, 22 (2006), 27–33.

— 'The study of medieval Irish castles: a bibliographic survey', *Proceedings of the Royal Irish Academy*, 108 (2008), 115–36.

Bence-Jones, Mark, *A guide to Irish country houses* (London, 1988).

Blades, Brooke S., 'English villages in the Londonderry plantation', *Post-medieval Archaeology*, 20 (1986), 257–69.

Bradley, John, & Ben Murtagh, 'Brady's Castle, Thomastown, Co. Kilkenny: a 14th-century fortified town house' in John R. Kenyon & Kieran O'Conor (eds), *The medieval castle in Ireland and Wales* (Dublin, 2003), pp 194–216.

Brady, Ciaran, 'Political women and reform in Tudor Ireland' in MacCurtain & O'Dowd (eds), *Women in early modern Ireland* (1991), pp 69–90.

Breen, Colin, *The Gaelic lordship of the O'Sullivan Beare* (Dublin, 2005).

Butler, W.F., 'The barony of Muskerry', *Journal of the Cork Historical and Archaeological Society*, 16 (1910), 81–8, 120–7.

Cairns, C.T., *Irish tower houses: a Co. Tipperary case study* (Dublin, 1987).

Canny, Nicholas, *From reformation to restoration: Ireland, 1534–1660* (Dublin, 1987).

— *Kingdom and colony: Ireland in the Atlantic world, 1560–1800* (Baltimore & London, 1988).

— 'Early modern Ireland, *c.*1500–1700' in Foster (ed.), *Oxford illustrated history of Ireland* (1989), pp 104–60.

Chinnery, Victor, 'Barryscourt refurbished: the reinstatement of a late sixteenth-century Irish domestic interior' in Ludlow & Jameson (eds), *Barryscourt lectures* (2004), pp 177–224.

Collins, J.T., 'Some McCarthys of Blarney and Ballea', *Journal of the Cork Historical and Archaeological Society*, 59 (1954), 1–10, 82–8.

— 'Some McCarthys of Blarney and Ballea', *Journal of the Cork Historical and Archaeological Society*, 60 (1955), 1–5, 75–9.

— 'The McCarthys of Muskerry and Blarney Castle', *Old Blarney: Journal of the Blarney and District Historical Society*, 4 (1999), 11–27.

Connolly, R.E., *If walls could talk: great Irish castles tell their stories* (Dublin, 2004).

Craig, Maurice, *The architecture of Ireland from the earliest times to 1880* (Portrane, Dublin, 1989).

Crawford Woods, Cecil, 'Blarney Castle, County Cork, double structure of its keep', *Journal of the Cork Historical and Archaeological Society*, 2 (1896), 337–44.

Crofton Croker, Thomas, *Researches in the south of Ireland* (London, 1824).

Cronin, Maura, 'Work and workers in Cork city and county, 1800–1900' in O'Flanagan & Buttimer (eds), *Cork, history and society* (1993), pp 721–58.

De Breffny, Brian, & George Mott, *Castles of Ireland* (London, 1977).

De Breffny, Brian, & Rosemary ffolliott, *The houses of Ireland* (London, 1975).

Donnelly, C.J., 'Sectionally constructed tower houses: a review of the evidence from County Limerick', *Journal of the Royal Society of Antiquaries of Ireland*, 128 (1998), 26–34.

— 'Tower houses and late medieval secular settlement in county Limerick' in Duffy, Edwards & FitzPatrick (eds), *Gaelic Ireland* (2001), pp 315–28.

Duffy, P.J., David Edwards & Elizabeth FitzPatrick (eds), *Gaelic Ireland, c.1250–c.1650: land, lordship and settlement* (Dublin, 2001).

Edwards, David, *The Ormond lordship in County Kilkenny, 1515–1642: the rise and fall of Butler feudal power* (Dublin, 2003).

Feehan, John, *Farming in Ireland* (Dublin, 2003).

Fenlon, Jane, *Goods & chattels: a survey of early household inventories in Ireland* (Dublin, 2003).

Fitzgerald, Walter, 'Notes on Sir John MacCoghlan, Knight of Cloghan, Chief of Delvin-MacCoghlan who died in 1590', *Journal of the Royal Society of Antiquaries of Ireland*, 43 (1913), 223–31.

FitzPatrick, Elizabeth, & Paul Walsh, 'Buildings and architecture' in Elizabeth FitzPatrick, Madeline O'Brien & Paul Walsh (eds), *Archaeological investigations in Galway City, 1987–1998* (Bray, 2004), pp 337–55.

Foster, R.F. (ed.), *The Oxford illustrated history of Ireland* (Oxford, 1989).

Gilchrist, Roberta, 'Ambivalent bodies: gender and medieval archaeology' in Jenny Moore & Eleanor Scott (eds), *Invisible people and processes: writing gender and childhood into European archaeology* (London & New York, 1997), pp 42–58.

— *Gender and archaeology: contesting the past* (London & New York, 1999).

Harbison, Peter (ed.), *Beranger's views of Ireland* (Dublin, 1991).

Harris, Neil, 'Selling national culture: Ireland at the World's Columbian Exposition' in T.J. Edelstein (ed.), *Imagining an Irish past: the Celtic Revival, 1840–1940* (Chicago, 1992), pp 82–105.

Hayes-McCoy, G.A., 'The Tudor conquest (1534–1603)' in Moody & Martin (eds), *The course of Irish history* (2001), pp 139–51.

Healy, J.N., *The castles of County Cork* (Cork, 1988).

Henderson, Paula, 'Life at the top: sixteenth- and seventeenth-century roofscapes', *Country Life*, 177 (1985), 6–9.

Howley, James, *The follies and garden buildings of Ireland* (New Haven & London, 1993).

J.C., 'Notes and queries', *Journal of the Cork Historical and Archaeological Society*, 20 (1914), 156–8.

Johnson, Matthew, *Behind the castle gate: from medieval to renaissance* (London & New York, 2002).

Jope, E.M., 'Moyry, Charlemont, Castleraw and Richhill: fortification to architecture in the north of Ireland, 1570–1700', *Ulster Journal of Archaeology*, 23 (1960), 97–123.

Jordan, A.J., 'Date, chronology and evolution of the County Wexford tower house', *Journal of the Wexford Historical Society*, 13 (1990–1), 30–81.

Kerrigan, P.M., *Castles and fortifications in Ireland, 1485–1945* (Cork, 1995).

Klingelhöfer, Eric, 'Edmund Spenser at Kilcolman Castle: the archaeological evidence', *Post-Medieval Archaeology*, 39:1 (2005), 133–54.

Leask, H.G., *Irish castles and castellated houses* (Dundalk, 1951).

— 'Early seventeenth-century houses in Ireland' in E.M. Jope (ed.), *Studies in building history: essays in recognition of the work of B.H. St John O'Neil* (London, 1961), pp 243–50.

Leerssen, Joep, *Mere Irish and Fíor Ghael: studies in the idea of Irish nationality, its development and literary expression prior to the nineteenth century* (Amsterdam & Philadelphia, 1986).

Lewis, Samuel, *A topographical dictionary of Ireland*, 2 vols (London, 1837; repr. New York, 1970).

Loeber, Rolf, 'Early Classicism in Ireland: architecture before the Georgian era', *Architectural History*, 22 (1979), 49–63.

— *The geography and practice of English colonization in Ireland from 1534 to 1609* (Athlone, 1991),

— 'An architectural history of Gaelic castles and settlements, 1370–1600' in Duffy, Edwards & FitzPatrick (eds), *Gaelic Ireland* (2001), pp 271–314.

Loeber, Rolf, & Magda Stouthamer-Loeber, 'The lost architecture of the Wexford Plantation' in Kevin Whelan & William Nolan (eds), *Wexford, history and society:*

interdisciplinary essays on the history of an Irish county (Dublin, 1987), pp 173–200.

Ludlow, John, & Noel Jameson (eds), *Medieval Ireland: the Barryscourt lectures I–X* (Kinsale, Cork, 2004).

Lydon, James, *The making of Ireland, from ancient times to the present* (London & New York, 1998).

MacCarthy-Morrogh, Michael, *The Munster Plantation: English migration to southern Ireland, 1583–1641* (Oxford, 1986).

MacCurtain, Margaret, & Mary O'Dowd (eds), *Women in early modern Ireland* (Dublin, 1991).

MacLysaght, Edward, *Irish life in the seventeenth century* (Shannon, 1969).

Maher, Denise, *Kilcrea Friary: Franciscan heritage in County Cork* (Cork, 1999).

Mahony, F.S., *The reliques of Father Prout* (London, 1860).

Martin, F.X., 'The Normans: arrival and settlement, 1169–*c*.1300' in Moody & Martin (eds), *Course of Irish history* (2001), pp 95–112.

McAuliffe, Mary, 'The lady in the tower: the social and political role of women in tower houses' in Meek & Simms (eds), *The fragility of her sex?* (1996), pp 153–62.

McCarthy, C.J.F., 'An antiquary's note book, 12', *Journal of the Cork Historical and Archaeological Society*, 95 (1990), 158–64.

McCarthy, W.P., 'The litigious earl', *Journal of the Cork Historical and Archaeological Society*, 70 (1965), 7–13.

McCullough, Niall, *Palimpsest: change in the Irish building tradition* (Dublin, 1994).

McKenna, Elizabeth, 'Was there a political role for women in medieval Ireland?' in Meek & Simms (eds), *The fragility of her sex?* (1996), pp 163–74.

McNeill, Tom, *Castles in Ireland: feudal power in a Gaelic world* (London & New York, 1997).

Meek, Christine, & Katharine Simms (eds), *The fragility of her sex? Medieval Irish women in their European context* (Dublin, 1996).

M.G., 'Notes and queries', *Journal of the Cork Historical and Archaeological Society*, 17 (1911), 35–6.

Moody, T.W., & F.X. Martin (eds), *The course of Irish history* (Dublin, 2001).

Morton, Karena, 'Irish medieval wall painting' in Ludlow & Jameson (eds), *Barryscourt lectures* (2004), pp 313–49.

Mosley, Charles, (ed.), *Burke's peerage & baronetage*, 2 vols (106th ed. London, 1999).

Mulcahy, John, 'The Church of Ireland in Blarney', *Old Blarney: Journal of the Blarney and District Historical Society*, 3 (1993), 42–54.

— 'The diplomatic career of Captain James Jefferyes, Blarney Castle', *Old Blarney: Journal of the Blarney and District Historical Society*, 6 (2002), 7–30.

Murphy, J.A., 'Cork: anatomy and essence' in O'Flanagan & Buttimer (eds), *Cork, history and society* (1993), pp 1–14.

Nicholls, K.W., 'The development of lordship in County Cork' in O'Flanagan & Buttimer (eds), *Cork, history and society* (1993), pp 157–211.
— 'Irishwomen and property in the sixteenth century' in MacCurtain & O'Dowd (eds), *Women in early modern Ireland* (1991), pp 17–31.
O'Callaghan, John, 'Fortified houses of the sixteenth century in south Wexford', *Journal of the Old Wexford Society*, 8 (1980–1), 1–51.
Ó Corráin, Donnchadh, *Ireland before the Normans* (Dublin, 1972).
O'Brien, A.F., 'Politics, economy and society: the development of Cork and the Irish south-coast region, *c.*1170 to *c.*1583' in O'Flanagan & Buttimer (eds), *Cork, history and society* (1993), pp 83–156.
Ó Danachair, Caoimhín, 'Irish tower houses and their regional distribution', *Bealoideas*, 45–7 (1977–9), 158–63.
O'Donovan, John (ed.), *Annals of the kingdom of Ireland by the Four Masters, from the earliest period to the year 1616*, 7 vols (Dublin, 1856; repr. Dublin, 1990).
O'Dowd, Mary, 'Gaelic economy and society' in Ciaran Brady & Raymond Gillespie (eds), *Natives and newcomers: the making of Irish colonial society, 1534–1641* (Dublin, 1986), pp 120–47.
O'Dwyer, Frederick, 'In search of Christopher Myers: pioneer of the Gothic revival in Ireland' in Michael McCarthy & Karina O'Neill (eds), *Studies in the Gothic Revival* (Dublin, 2008), pp 51–111.
O'Flanagan, Patrick, 'Three hundred years of urban life: villages and towns in County Cork, *c.*1600 to 1901' in O'Flanagan & Buttimer (eds), *Cork, history and society* (1993), pp 391–467.
O'Flanagan, Patrick, & C.G. Buttimer (eds), *Cork, history and society: interdisciplinary essays on the history of an Irish county* (Dublin, 1993).
O'Grady, Standish (ed.), *Pacata Hibernia, or History of the wars in Ireland during the reign of Queen Elizabeth*, 2 vols (London, 1896).
—, *Caithreim Thoirdelbhaigh*, 2 vols (Dublin, 1929).
O'Keeffe, Tadhg, *Medieval Ireland: an archaeology* (Stroud, Gloucestershire, 2000).
— 'Barryscourt castle and the Irish tower-house' in Ludlow & Jameson (eds), *Barryscourt lectures* (2004), pp 3–31.
— 'Concepts of "castle" and the construction of identity in medieval and post-medieval Ireland', *Irish Geography*, 34:1 (2001), 69–88.
— 'Space, place, habitus: geographies of practice in an Anglo-Norman manor' in Howard B. Clarke, Jacinta Prunty & Mark Hennessy (eds), *Surveying Ireland's past: multidisciplinary essays in honour of Anngret Simms* (Dublin, 2004), pp 73–98.
O'Mahony, Colman, 'Bygone industries of Blarney and Dripsey', *Journal of Cork Historical and Archaeological Society*, 89 (1984), 77–87.
Ó Murchadha, Diarmuid, *Family names of County Cork* (Cork, 1996).
O'Sullivan, C.M., *Hospitality in medieval Ireland, 900–1500* (Dublin, 2004).

Pollock, Dave, 'The bawn exposed: recent excavations at Barryscourt' in Ludlow & Jameson (eds), *Barryscourt lectures* (2004), pp 145–75.

— 'The Barryscourt hall and the remains of some other medieval timber buildings' in Conleth Manning (ed.), *From ringforts to fortified houses: studies on castles and other monuments in honour of David Sweetman* (Bray, 2007), pp 261–72.

Power, Denis, with Elizabeth Byrne, Ursula Egan, Sheila Lane & Mary Sleeman, *Archaeological inventory of County Cork. Vol. 2: east and south-Cork* (Dublin, 1994).

—, *Archaeological inventory of County Cork. Vol. 3: mid-Cork* (Dublin, 1997).

Power, Denis, Sheila Lane, Elizabeth Byrne, Ursula Egan, Mary Sleeman, Eamonn Cotter & Judith Monk, *Archaeological inventory of County Cork. Vol. 4: north Cork, part 2* (Dublin, 2000).

Quane, Michael, 'Tour in Ireland by John Harden in 1797', *Journal of the Cork Historical and Archaeological Society*, 60 (1955), 80–7.

Quinn, David B., 'The Munster Plantation: problems and opportunities', *Journal of the Cork Historical and Archaeological Society*, 71 (1966), 19–40.

Ronnes, Hanneke, *Architecture and elite culture in the United Provinces, England and Ireland, 1500–1700* (Amsterdam, 2006).

— 'Continental traces at Carrick-on-Suir and contemporary Irish castles: a preliminary study of date-and-initial stones' in Thomas Herron and Michael Potterton (eds), *Ireland in the Renaissance, c.1540–1660* (Dublin, 2007), pp 253–73.

Rooney, B., 'The Irish Exibition at Olympia, 1888', *Irish Architectural and Decorative Studies*, 1 (1998), 101–19.

Rutherford, A.G., 'A social interpretation of the castle in Scotland' (PhD, U. Glasgow, 1998).

Salter, Mike, *The castles of south Munster* (Malvern, Worcs, 2004).

Samson, Ross, 'The rise and fall of tower houses in post-Reformation Scotland' in Ross Samson (ed.), *The social archaeology of houses* (Edinburgh, 1990), pp 197–243.

Samuel, Mark, & Kate Hamlyn, *Blarney Castle: its history, development and purpose* (Cork, 2007).

Sherlock, Rory, 'Cross-cultural occurrences of mutations in tower house architecture', *Journal of Irish Archaeology*, 15 (2006), 73–91.

— 'The evolution of the Irish tower house as a domestic space', *Proceedings of the Royal Irish Academy*, 111C (2010), 115–40.

Shirley, E.P. et al., 'Extracts from the journal of Thomas Dineley, Esquire, giving some account of his visit to Ireland in the reign of Charles II', *Journal of the Kilkenny and South-East of Ireland Archaeological Society*, 6 (1867), 73–91.

Simington, R.C. (ed.), *The Civil Survey, AD1654–1656: County of Waterford. Vol. VI with appendices: Muskerry Barony, Co. Cork …* (Dublin, 1942).

Simms, Katharine, *From kings to warlords: the changing political structure of Gaelic Ireland in the later Middle Ages* (Woodbridge & Wolfeboro, 1987).

— 'Native sources for Gaelic settlement: the house poems' in Duffy, Edwards & FitzPatrick (eds), *Gaelic Ireland* (2001), pp 246–67.

Simpson, J.A., & E.S.C. Weiner, *The Oxford English dictionary*, 20 vols (2nd ed. Oxford, 1989).

Smith, Charles, *The ancient and present state of the county and city of Cork …* (Cork, 1750, 1893 ed.).

Sweetman, David, *Medieval castles of Ireland* (Cork, 1999).

— 'The origin and development of the tower house in Ireland' in Ludlow & Jameson (eds), *Barryscourt lectures* (2004), pp 261–87.

Thompson, M.W., *The decline of the castle* (Cambridge, 1987).

Weadick, Sharon, 'How popular were fortified houses in Irish castle building history? A look at their numbers in the archaeological record and distribution patterns' in James Lyttleton and Colin Rynne (eds), *Plantation Ireland: settlement and material culture, c.1550–c.1700* (Dublin, 2009), pp 61–85.

Webb Gillman, Herbert, 'Carrignamuck Castle, County Cork: a stronghold of the MacCarthys', *Journal of the Cork Historical and Archaeological Society*, 1 (1892), 11–19, 30–7.

— 'Sir Cormac McTeige MacCarthy and the sept lands of Muskerry, Co. Cork; with a historical pedigree', *Journal of the Cork Historical and Archaeological Society*, 1 (1892), 193–200.

Westropp, T.J., 'The ancient castles of the County of Limerick', *Proceedings of the Royal Irish Academy*, 26C (1907), 55–108.

Williams, Jeremy, *A companion guide to architecture in Ireland, 1837–1921* (Dublin, 1994).

Williamson, Tom, *Polite landscapes, gardens and society in eighteenth-century England* (Baltimore, MD, 1995).

Young, Arthur, *A tour in Ireland with general observations on the present state of that kingdom made in the years 1776, 1777 and 1778* (repr. Cambridge, 1925).

Glossary

Alure	Walkway along castle battlements
Ancone	Stone projection that supports or appears to support an entablature
Annals	Record of historic events year by year, such as battles and obituaries of members of the nobility
Ashlar	Dressed blocks of stone for building, laid in regular courses
Bawn	Walled courtyard of a tower house, commonly provided with gatehouse and corner towers (word originates from the Irish *bádhun* or cattle fort – an enclosure where cattle could be corralled)
Bell-cote	A structure of stone or timber placed on top of a building in which a bell is hung
Byre	Outhouse on farm
Centring	Frame used to support an arch under construction. In tower houses, it was common to use wicker mats to give shape to the arch. Once the mortar had dried and the arch had set in place, the centring was removed, leaving behind the impression of the wicker mats in the mortar
Chamfer	Where the right-angled edge of the stone has been cut away to create a third face
Chiefry	Office or territory of a Gaelic-Irish lord
Columbarium	Niches within the walls of a dovecot that contained the birds' nests
Console	Stone projections that support or appear to support an entablature
Crenellation	The battlements or parapets of a castle punctuated with regular openings along the top of the wall
Demesne	The country estate of a lord
Entablature	The upper part of a classical structure supported by columns
Flanker	Towers, typically circular or rectilinear, placed at the corners of bawns to cover their perimeter
Garderobe	Toilet chamber in medieval building
Harling	Lime-based mortar covering used to protect external surfaces of walls
Lintel	Horizontal support (timber or stone) across top of window or doorway
Loop	Small narrow window, typically found in castles

Machicolation	Stone structure projecting externally from top of castle façade. Supported by a line of arches or corbels. Protected castle occupants dropping stones etc. from holes in between the arches or corbels onto attackers at the base of the wall
Merlon	The solid portion of a crenellated parapet
Mullion	A vertical stone or timber dividing a window into separate lights
Newel	Central pillar or post from which the steps of a spiral stairs project
Ogee	Double curve, partially concave, partially convex – commonly seen in window heads
Ope	Opening, typically a window or loop
Oriel	Bay window projecting from upper floor, supported by corbelling
Sept	A branch of a Gaelic-Irish family
Soffit	Underside of an arch
Spall	Small stones used to fill in gaps in between the larger stones of an irregularly coursed wall
Spandrel	The triangular space between the outside curve of an arch and its surrounding rectilinear frame
Suzerainty	Control by one territory over another
Transom	A horizontal stone or timber dividing a window into separate lights
Wall-walk	Walkway along the battlements or parapets of a castle
Yett	Iron grille that could be closed in front of the entrance into a tower house

Index

Note: page numbers in **_bold italics_** refer to illustrations.

MacCarthy, Cormac Óg mac Cormaic Óig,
    first viscount Muskerry, 12–13, 107–8,
    114
MacCarthy, Sir Cormac Óg mac Diarmada,
    5, 8, 10, 11, 12
MacCarthy, Diarmaid mac Taidhg, 7
MacCarthy, Diarmait, king of Desmond, 1
MacCarthy, Donnchadh mac Cormaic Óig,
    earl of Clancarty, 13–15
MacCarthy, Donough mac Callaghan, earl
    of Clancarty, 15, 17
MacCarthy, Eóghan mac Taidhg, 5
MacCarthy, Julia, 118
MacCarthy, Tadhg mac Cormaic, 5
MacCarthy, Tadhg mac Cormaic Óig, 7, 118
MacCarthy lordship, 2, 3, 5, 6, 35, 100, 103,
    112
    consolidation of, 91
    decline of power, 7–12
    earls of Clancarty, 14, 15, 17, 108, 119
    as landlords, 12–17
    social status, 44
MacCarthy Mór, 2, 93
MacCarthy Reagh, 2
MacCoghlan, Sir John, 77
MacDonagh-MacCarthys, 2
MacEgan, Solomon, 77
machicolation, **82**, **83**, 85, 99, 114, 125
McNeill, Tom, 30
Macosquin, Co. Derry, 42
Macroom, Co. Cork, 14, 15, 16, 108, 119
Maguire, Cuconnaught, 11
Mahony, Francis Sylvester ('Fr Prout'), 12
Mallow, Co. Cork, 100
manor houses, 29, 100–8, 119
    dating, 102–3
Martin river, 37, 116
Mary I, Queen of England, 92
megalithic tombs, mock, 18, **19**, 108
Mellifont, Treaty of, 1603, 9
monasteries, 32
Monivea, Co. Galway, 34
Monkstown, Co. Cork, 56, 100, **102**, 118
Moryson, Fynes, 31
Mourne Abbey, Co. Cork, 5, 112

Munster, 10, 71
    Anglo-Normans in, 1–2
    MacCarthy lordships, 6
    plantation, 12
    tower houses, 28, 79, 80
murder-holes, 51
Muskerry, 5, 6, 20, 35, 103, 108
    borders, 112, 114
    Gaelic lordships decline, 7–12
Myrtle Grove, Co. Cork, 76

Napoleonic Wars, 21
Nenagh, Co. Tipperary, **27**
New English, 100
Newcastlewest, Co. Limerick, 104
Nine Years War, 8, 9, 10, 12, 58

Ó Cléirigh, Mícheál, 32
Ó Danachair, Caoimhín, 26
Ó Domhnaill, Conn, 76
O'Brien, Donnchadh, 95
O'Brien, Mór, 95
O'Briens, 1, 6
O'Connor, Turlough, 1
O'Connor Faly, 92
O'Dalys, 2
O'Donnell, Red Hugh, earl of Tyrconnell, 9
O'Donnell, Rory, earl of Tyrconnell, 11
O'Driscolls, 2
Offaly, County, 77, 92, 102
O'Flahertys, 104
Ó hUiginn, Tadhg Dall, 76
Old English, 100
O'Maddens, 33
O'Mahonys, 2, 20, 22
O'Neill, Aodh, 94
O'Neill, Gormlaith, 94–5
O'Neill, Hugh, earl of Tyrone, 8, 9, 10–11
O'Neill, Turlough Luineach, 92
Ordnance Survey, 25
Ormond, 'Black Tom', tenth earl of, 58
Ormond, duke of, 15
Ormond, lordship of, 3, 10, 118
Ormond Castle, Co. Tipperary, 58
Orrery, earl of, 103